What We Say

Is What We Get!

D1521612

The Keys to Building
Good Communication Skills for Successful Living

"Gerald has taken on a subject that affects everyone—the art of communication. He is able to master the intricacy of providing valuable information, similar to a self-help book, and include real-life experiences and entertainment. He touches on sensitive areas—couple relationships, parent-child relationships, employer-employee relationships—and provides insight into how effective communication can prevail. Gerald also provides tools for readers to utilize in order to enhance their own communication levels. This book is an inspiration to those who want to improve their relationships with others."

Mary Jo Werner, CPA-Attorney, WIPFLI Accounting

GERALD BALDNER

NELSON BOOKS
Elgin, IL

To order additional copies of this book, please call Gerald Baldner's company Kitchen Solvers at 800-845-6779, or send an e-mail to gerald@kitchensolvers.com.

Published by Nelson Books
P.O. Box 5394
Elgin, IL 60123

Publisher's Cataloging-in-Publication Data
Baldner, Gerald

   What we say is what we get! : the keys to building good communication skills for successful living / by Gerald Baldner. --Elgin, Ill. : Nelson Books, 2003.

   p. ; cm.

   ISBN: 0-9742601-0-X

   1. Communication. 2. Interpersonal communication. 3. Business communication. I. Title.

P90 .B35 2003   2003108432
302.2--dc21   0308

Book coordination by Jenkins Group, Inc. • www.bookpublishing.com
Cover design by Leslie Tane
Interior design by Fourteen Little Men, Inc.

Printed in the United States of America

07 06 05 04 03 • 5 4 3 2 1

Dedication

I would like to dedicate this book to my mother and father who taught me the value of developing and maintaining meaningful relationships; to my wife Betty, who has given me the privilege of experiencing the ultimate meaning of love; and to my four children, Tami, Jody, Leslie and Jason, who have given me the opportunity to experience the rewards of reciprocal love.

I love and respect you with all my heart.

Acknowledgments

Writing this book has been an interesting journey for me. Traveling down a road that you have never traveled before has its share of ups and downs, twists and turns. I have many people to thank for making this journey a positive experience.

I would like to thank the following people for letting me interview them in regards to their thoughts, emotions and experiences about communication. Thank you to Faythe Kalkwarf, Lindy Saline, Rev. Vern Rice, Bergitta Rice, Audrey Clausen, Jeanne Plunkett, Mark Solyst, Leslie Baldner, Tim Carlson, Anne Steuer, Steve Plopper, David Amborn, Carol Payant and Dave Woggan. The time you gave and the input you provided was extremely valuable to me, and I appreciate it.

Thank you to my daughters Jody Lyon and Tami Nabor who, during the early stages of the project, shared their editing expertise.

I am very appreciative of the time and interest that two good friends, Jeanne Plunkett and Tim Carlson, gave to the effort in editing and commenting on every word I wrote in its original form. Thank you for your time and especially your friendship.

Special thanks go to Dr. Richard Morehouse, Professor of Psychology at Viterbo University. He and his students managed to find time, even with their other classwork, to collect and compile communication surveys for me, with Dr. Morehouse extrapolating some interesting information from the results.

I particularly want to thank my wife Betty for all the encouragement she gave me throughout the entire journey. I am most appreciative for the time and effort it took for her to decipher my handwriting, and for her initial typing and editing of that written manuscript.

My last acknowledgment and thank you goes to my good friend Judy Kirkpatrick. During the early stages of this project, I had a lot of thoughts and ideas that I knew I wanted to communicate. At times, I struggled with how to say these things in a clear and meaningful way. Then, in the middle of the night, it came to me—Judy! Judy Kirkpatrick is well known in our community for her creative mind and intellect. And besides that, she is just a very nice person. Judy agreed to edit and refine my words, and I do not believe this book would have become a reality without her help. Thank you, Judy, for the endless hours that you devoted to editing my words, smoothing out the rough spots, and for all the hours we spent discussing what we thought would be appealing to the reader. We also shared a lot of laughter, didn't we? Thank you very much for everything you did, every thought you shared, your encouragement and, most of all, for being my friend.

Gerald Baldner
La Crosse, Wisconsin
April 2003

CONTENTS

PROLOGUE

Communication. Communication is an exchange of thoughts, words, feelings and emotions between people. The way we communicate with others and how others communicate with us can cause positive and negative feelings. This is not to say that every time we use some form of communication it generates some emotional response. In fact, in most cases it does not. However, most of this book will deal with those experiences of communication that do spawn positive or negative emotions and how they impact our lives and the lives of those around us.

Have you ever thought about—I mean *really thought about*—what kind of a communicator you are? Do you give serious consideration to what kind of first impression you make with people? I strongly suspect that the degree to which this book appeals to you will depend on how important the art of communication is to you.

In essence, how we communicate has a great deal to do with how others describe our personality. If someone says of someone else "they have a great personality," he/she probably is describing how that person communicates, how he/she "comes across" in personal interactions. A "bubbly personality" may mean someone is upbeat and outgoing when they talk. "He's standoffish and intimidating" can mean someone communicates in an arrogant and unforgiving way. The personality we project is determined by the way we communicate with others.

Consider this hypothesis: The way we communicate with others reflects what kind of personality we have. In turn, our personality determines how many friends we have or how well we get along with our families, friends, co-workers and peers. In turn, how well we get along with these people who come into our lives determines how happy we are. If you agree with this analogy, then probably you will agree that *What We Say Is What We Get.*

In our personal, social, and family relationships, success might be measured by how many positive, meaningful relationships we have or by how rewarding the relationships are for us. Clear communication smoothes out so many of the bumps in life's road for us and our loved ones.

In business, our communication skills can be more evident. Good, positive communication skills often are rewarded by promotions, financial bonuses or both. People who are able to communicate well on all levels often find themselves in leadership roles.

Successful communication in our spiritual relationships is more personal, subjective, and difficult to describe. They are as unique and individual as each person is unique and individual. In the chapter on *"The Ultimate Relationship,"* I will try to explain what it means to me.

In order to lead a happy and fulfilling life, I believe it is important to seek success in all areas of your life. In my own life, I know people who appear to be happy in certain areas of their lives but are very unhappy or dissatisfied in others. It is also apparent to me that some people put a much higher priority on attaining success in one area of their lives over another, e.g., career before family or financial gains before spiritual contentment. I would encourage you to work at maintaining a balance of happy or satisfied feelings in all areas of life.

Also be aware that communication skills can fluctuate from one relationship setting to another. Some people do better communicating in business settings, while others are at their best on a personal level. I believe people who are the most consistent in their communication styles in all settings are the happiest and most likely to achieve and enjoy successful living.

When writing a non-fiction book, the author must acknowledge that he/she will be making statements or promoting beliefs that may not be held true by everyone. So it is with this book. What is important for you to remember is that the words, thoughts and statements in this book are what *I* believe to be true. They may not reflect what you believe, and, if you choose to continue reading (and my publisher and I hope you do!), please feel free to disagree with me. I do not profess to know everything there is to know about communications and how to build positive relationships. Certainly, while I have enjoyed many positive relationships in my lifetime, others have been less fulfilling. Yet that is the wonderful thing about our attempts at communication. Each daily encounter with people, whether old friends, co-workers, or new acquaintances, gives us an opportunity to practice and improve our communication skills. We can see the results of our efforts almost immediately. No need to lose 25 lbs. or work out at a gym for 6 weeks or complete a semester course. Communication is immediate, and enhancing your communication skills can be immediately apparent.

It is my hope that together we can give new meaning to how we relate to one another. If you are able to improve your relationships with other people, then we have been successful. I hope to maintain your interest, and communicate with you in an honest, from-the-heart style.

When we look into a mirror, we see ourselves as others see us. We see our size and shape. We see the way our clothes coordinate or clash. We can take a good look at our hair, our make-up, our posture and our smile. If we look into that mirror with the intention of making the best possible visible impression, we can make changes—positive changes that will give us confidence.

This book can serve as a "communication mirror," a way to see yourself differently than you have ever seen yourself before. Ideally, you will identify with some of the examples shared that will confirm and enhance your own patterns of communication. Perhaps you will see a crack in your communication mirror, a reflected flaw in the way you communicate that you will want to repair.

Over the past 30 years, I have read many self-help books. Frequently, I learned something from the author's thoughts. Sometimes I would recognize my faults and weaknesses and attempt to correct them. There would also be those times when the author would positively confirm my own behavior, letting me know I was "on the right track."

I consider this book to be a self-help book. It is my goal to heighten your awareness of your own communication style. As I have laid the groundwork to write this book, I have made discoveries about myself and my own ability to communicate.

Some of those discoveries pleased me; some did not.

I discovered that often I am unable to keep emotions out of my communications, which can make a tense situation worse. I've discovered that even though I rarely retreat from controversy, I certainly do not care for conflict (to be more precise, I hate it!). That, in turn, makes me work harder at communicating more clearly to avoid any misunderstanding or controversy that might arise. Returning to the communication mirror analogy, I've discovered a couple of bits of spinach in my teeth and I am going to have to work to get rid of them! As I write, I wonder what *you* are going to see in that mirror and if we can work together to make improvements.

CHAPTER ONE

Getting In Shape

Where I've Been and the Role Communication has Played in My Success

---

An engineer, a mathematician, and a physicist were standing around the college flagpole when an English professor happened by.

"What are you doing?" asked the newcomer.

"We need to know the height of the flagpole," explained the engineer, "and we're discussing the various formulas and equations we might use to calculate it."

The English professor studied the situation for a moment, then pulled the pole from its base, laid it on the ground, borrowed a tape measure and announced "It's 24 feet exactly."

He put the pole back and walked away.

"English professors," sneered the mathematician. "We ask him for the height and he gives us the length."

There's more than one way to see things!

Getting In Shape

n some ways, I have been a student of communication most of my life. Many experiences from my life's journey thus far have helped to shape the way in which I communicate today, teaching and illustrating for me the best—and sometimes the worst—ways to communicate. Who I am and what I am *today* is the direct result of these experiences. I emphasize *today* because each new experience may impact me in such a way that it could change the way I communicate with others from this day forward.

Indulge me, if you would, while I tell you a little bit of my history and explain briefly how it has contributed to the way I communicate today. (I urge you to think about your own life and see if you can do the same.)

I was born and raised on a small farm in Iowa, nurtured by two loving parents who cared very much about their three children. I have one sister four years older than me and a twin sister (who happens to be 10 minutes older and never misses an opportunity to remind me of that fact). By today's standards, we probably would have been considered poor; however, I never felt deprived. My parents instilled a sense of pride in us and taught us not to be afraid of hard work and to take pride in our accomplishments individually and as a family.

It was very important for me to be well liked, and I worked hard at trying to be nice to people, following the tenets of the Golden Rule with great fervor. I wanted to be treated kindly and with respect, so I treated everyone else that way.

My parents were excellent role models, and though dissimilar and distinct in their personalities, in complete accord as a couple. Mother was the outgoing, social lady, enthusiastic in everything she did and excited by everything happening around her. She could meet people for the first time and make them instantly comfortable by her interest in them. Father, on the other hand, was quiet, a man of few words, but an exceptionally good listener. Whether it was a neighbor's temperamental tractor, a daughter's boyfriend problem, or simply a stranger's comments on Iowa farming, he would listen with the same concern and put the speaker in the center of his world. Watching their interactions with people and seeing how much they enjoyed each exchange, how could I not follow my parents' examples as I grew?

Early in high school I discovered I had the ability to build positive relationships by showing a sincere interest in other people. Of course, I just thought I was being friendly and polite! Classmates (particularly girls!) informed me that I was easy to talk to and would share with me their own concerns, conflicts, and general feelings. As a result of their trust in me, I found myself in leadership roles, serving as president of five different organizations during my senior year in high school, including president of our student body. I was very active in athletics, lettering in four sports that final year. Certainly, being a part of athletic teams and organized groups made a positive contribution to what I was learning about communication (again, I just thought I was being friendly, polite and having a good time!).

Following high school, I attended Wartburg College in Waverly, Iowa. Although Wartburg was a relatively small private college, our class was much larger than high school and I suffered "small fish-bigger pond" syndrome, fearful that I would not experience the same level of popularity as I had in high school. This led me to try altering my style of communication. I learned to swear! Pretty heavy stuff in those days. It succeeded in getting people's attention, but it just wasn't me…and besides, I kept waiting to hear my father's disapproving and cautioning "Gerald!" each time I swore. Often, I would be so focused on using unfamiliar curse words that I would lose my point of reference and forget exactly what it was I was trying to communicate in the first place! I discovered what almost everyone in the world discovers at some time—you just cannot be someone you are not!

As time went on, I found that the same pattern of communication I had used in high school (i.e., showing sincere interest in people) paid off again, and I developed many close friends and lasting relationships at Wartburg. It was there that I met Betty Kalkwarf, my bride-to-be. Through my long and enduring friendship with this remarkable woman (38 years of marriage), I have learned the most about the importance of communicating, something we'll examine closer in Chapter Five.

Although undecided on a major when I first arrived on the college scene, I later decided to become a social worker, in part because of the many late night sessions I'd spent talking to my friends about their problems. It was, as they say, "a good fit." Betty and I were married the summer after we graduated in 1965. I then enrolled at the University of Utah in Salt Lake City to work on my Master's Degree in Social Work, while Betty secured a position teaching French to seventh, eighth and ninth grade students.

While this is beginning to sound like pure autobiography, I think it is important that you understand where I am coming from in order to apply a sense of credibility to my words—my working credentials, if you will.

After receiving my Master's in Social Work, I was entitled to be paid for what I used to do on a fairly regular basis in college! It led me to employment as a school social worker for grades K-12, first in Salt Lake City and then in Elkader, Iowa. While in Salt Lake, I also juggled being Admissions Director at a private boy's school and working as Youth Director with a local Lutheran church.

Out of these experiences grew a private practice as a marriage and family counselor. The one common theme that ran through counseling sessions (whether with married couples, troubled children, or confused adults) was that communication was important and *successful* communication was critical. No matter the problem, communication was needed. I also learned that no matter what the problem was, people couldn't change until they really wanted to, and even then there were no guarantees. In general, however, people can make positive changes if they have the desire to do so and are willing to work at making those changes.

During the first ten years of our marriage, Betty and I were blessed with four wonderful children, three daughters and a son. I loved the early stages of their lives, watching them grow, develop and, yes, communicate. The latter was fascinating to me. They would imitate words, phrases and gestures from Betty and me. It was a delightful surprise to realize that we were the most important people in our children's lives, and that what we did influenced them, even when we weren't aware of it.

Of course, we had the same challenges that most parents face as their children enter and emerge from adolescence, but comparatively speaking, we "lucked out" with our children. Today our kids are well-adjusted, self-sufficient adults of whom we are very proud. Communicating with them as adults is very different from what we went through when they were younger—but I loved every minute of it and now get to repeat those same delights with grandchildren!

In the chapter that deals with communicating with children, I'll pull out plenty of verbal snapshots of my children to illustrate what works—and doesn't work—in communication.

Let's jump ahead several years to what turned out to be a major turning point in our lives. I was enjoying my professional role in social work, becoming involved in administration and then as a college professor in two different colleges in La Crosse, Wisconsin. Yet there was something missing, and I confess it was partially monetary. We were financially comfortable, but the salary structure of academic life is rather rigid. Okay, it's completely inflexible. At the beginning of each contract year, I knew how much money I'd be making, regardless of how much I worked or the quality of my work. Whatever position you hold in life, there should be rewards for diligence, commitment and hard work. A salary totally dependent upon level of education and years of service has a tendency to reward and even foster complacency and apathy.

In a definite life-altering move, I decided to pursue what had been, for many years, a yearning to run my own business, to find something requiring hard work and a challenge, two things my parents had taught me never to avoid. If it turned out to be financially rewarding, so much the better!

In the last 25 years, I have started eight different businesses. While that may seem like I can't hold a steady job, all but one of those businesses is successfully operating today. Those different business ventures have included manufacturing facilities where I hired employees, real estate investments with clients and tenants, retail ventures with direct sales to customers, and finally, franchising which deals with both employees and franchisees.

I have had several different business partners, and I can say from experience that communicating with business associates presents a whole new level of communication challenge. In some way, having multiple business partners is similar to being a polygamist. I have never understood how someone could successfully communicate with more than one wife at a time. In fact, there are great similarities in communication with spouses and business partners, and we'll look at that more closely in a later chapter.

The reason I bring up these various businesses is that I have learned, sometimes the hard way, how best to communicate with people on many levels. It doesn't matter how terrific the product is, how wonderful the opportunity may be—if I am unable to communicate and convey ideas clearly, no one will buy my products, join my business, or complete their assignments. Learning to communicate effectively is critical to making a business survive and be successful.

The business "marriage" that I want to mention briefly, and the one to which I have been the most dedicated for the past twenty years, is Kitchen Solvers.

Betty and I started Kitchen Solvers out of our home in 1982. It began as a small retail business for remodeling kitchens and bathrooms. We experienced a good degree of success during our first two years of operation and began to realize that we could successfully develop relationships with employees while maintaining mutual respect for each other.

A brief look backward: Early in my life, I made it a practice to listen and learn from others who were more accomplished and successful than I. It certainly paid off! While attending a large family dinner, I found myself seated across the table from someone who had started a small business and expanded it through a unique business vehicle called "franchising." It immediately struck a positive chord with me and served as a springboard for expanding our own business.

As of December 2002, we have 130 franchises throughout the United States and Canada. Our corporate office has eight employees and we have had no turnover of key employees in eleven years. I learned a great deal about the value of good communication while building franchisor-franchisee relationships, and the importance of developing compatibility and camaraderie with employees during the past 20 years. Kitchen Solvers is a wonderful business and I truly enjoy my relationships with our franchises, our employees, and my partners.

In an effort to discover how other people feel about communication, I conducted in-depth interviews with almost 20 individuals. Then, under the direction and supervision of Dr. Richard Morehouse, Professor of Psychology at Viterbo University, 200 additional people completed a communication survey. *(The results of these interview/surveys can be found in "Appendix i" and provide some interesting insights into people's perceptions of communication.)*

The individual interviews were so enjoyable! In most cases, people said that I asked them questions they had never really taken the time to consider seriously. I honestly believe that, as part of the process, the conscious effort they made in answering my questions gave them new and interesting insight into their own communication patterns.

I asked each person if it was important how other people communicated with him or her. Each person gave me an emphatic "Yes!" I was surprised that some individuals who I had assumed would have little concern about their own communication skills actually *did* have concern. Almost all the people I talked with had, at some point in their lives, made a personal effort at improving their communication skills. They all thought it was possible to improve communication habits. For the most part, I discovered that they enjoyed being asked questions about this significant yet often overlooked part of their lives. With most of the questions, their responses were not immediate. They took their time and explored their feelings before giving a thoughtful and often insightful answer.

Here are the questions I asked. It might be enjoyable and interesting to sit down with a friend or family member and discuss your own responses to these questions.

1. Do you think very often about how you communicate with other people and how they communicate with you?

2. Are there certain situations when you find it difficult to communicate? Why?

3. Who is someone that you think is a good communicator and why?

4. Do you communicate with other people differently than you do to the members of your family? Why?

5. Who are the most difficult people for you to communicate with? Why?

6. How important is it to you how other people communicate with you?

7. Have you ever made a conscious effort to improve your communication skills?

8. Do you believe it is possible for people to improve how they communicate?

9. If you could improve one thing about the way you communicate, what would it be?

As I asked these questions, I asked people to expand on their answers and, where possible, to give me some personal examples of what made them feel the way they did.

It has become increasingly apparent to me that we all have several different styles of communication that we select in our relationships. We do not necessarily communicate the same way to our spouse as we do with an employee, or to our children the same way we do with our friends. It is important to understand how these styles differ and why.

In different chapters, we'll take an in-depth look at how we communicate with others in a variety of situations. The chapters are not necessarily in any order of importance. In fact, it is not necessary that you read this book from front to back. If you feel like jumping ahead to some particular chapter that has special meaning for you, then by all means do so.

I hope this book will prove to be a positive step in your life's journey. Life is special, and how we communicate to one another has a great deal to do with how happy or unhappy we are in that life. If you are unhappy in any area of your life, maybe you need a communication "check-up." As an integral part of that communication check-up, I can emphatically tell you this: it is more important for you to evaluate how you communicate with others than for you to dwell on how others communicate with you.

I do believe with all my heart and mind that good communication skills can help you achieve and enjoy a successful life.

CHAPTER TWO

On Your Mark

So You Think it's Time to Take a Look at Your Communication Skills!

The company commander and his first sergeant were in the field and had gone to bed for the night.

After some time, the sergeant woke up the officer and said, "Sir, pardon my waking you, but would you look up and tell me what you see?"

The officer replied, "I see millions of stars."

"And what does that tell you?" asked the sergeant.

"Astronomically, it tells me that there are millions of galaxies and potentially billions of planets. Theologically, it tells me that God is great and we are small. Meteorologically, it tells me that tomorrow will be beautiful. What does it tell you, sergeant?"

The sergeant sighed.

"It tells me somebody has stolen our tent."

It's all in how you look at things, isn't it?

On Your Mark

How many people have you communicated with today? Yesterday? Last week? When you think about it, it is amazing, isn't it? Of all those people with whom you communicated, how did you feel about the words that were exchanged? Did you say something that you wish you could take back? Did someone say something to you that made you feel good or bad? How did you respond? Do most of the people you communicate with understand you? Are they sensitive to your feelings and emotions? Are you responsive to theirs?

These are some of the questions that I hope you will ask yourself and answer through an analysis of your own communication skills.

Indeed, we do communicate with many people every day. Of course, by the nature of their jobs, size of families, or the community they live in, etc., some people communicate with many more people than others.

It is my sincere desire that from this day forward each of you will become more aware of the impact your words and gestures have on others. How you communicate with other people and how other people communicate with you have a lot to do with how you feel at the end of the day. If you are anything like me, often you think back on the events of the day. Frequently, I review some of the more important conversations that I had during that time. When I revisit good conversations, I smile. If I recall negative or uncomfortable exchanges, I get an uneasy feeling in the pit of my stomach and try to think about what, if anything, I could or should have said differently.

I don't think it would be presumptuous of me to assume that you purchased this book because you have a sincere interest in how you communicate and how others communicate with you. With that assumption in mind, I want to share with you some very practical ideas on how you can evaluate your own communication skills. In some cases, you may not need to improve the way you interact with others, and many of the following suggestions will represent an affirmation of your own social skills. In other cases, you just might find some ideas or thoughts that make sense to you.

I am also making the assumption that everyone has an innate desire to be well-liked by others. The desire to be liked by others represents the single most important incentive in trying to improve communication skills. If someone should happen not to care how other people feel, I am afraid this book will have very little value.

So I encourage you to ask yourself this very simple question: "Is it important to me how other people feel about me?" If the answer is "yes," what can you do on a regular basis to achieve and accomplish that objective? Do you think that people should like you just the way you are and that you shouldn't have to make any special effort? Do you think others should make a conscious effort to treat you in such a way that will encourage you to like them? How you answer these questions has a lot to say about what kind of interpersonal relationships you have. Obviously, all relationships are not equal. Some relationships have a lot more meaning and are much more important to you than others. On the following pages, I am going to ask you to take some time to contemplate some of the questions I have asked and formulate some answers for yourself.

Who are the ten most important family members in my life?

	I feel good about my relationship to them	Our relationship could be improved
1. _____	☐	☐
2. _____	☐	☐
3. _____	☐	☐
4. _____	☐	☐
5. _____	☐	☐
6. _____	☐	☐
7. _____	☐	☐
8. _____	☐	☐
9. _____	☐	☐
10. _____	☐	☐

Who are the ten most important non-family members in my life?

	I feel good about my relationship to them	Our relationship could be improved
1. _____	☐	☐
2. _____	☐	☐
3. _____	☐	☐
4. _____	☐	☐
5. _____	☐	☐
6. _____	☐	☐
7. _____	☐	☐
8. _____	☐	☐
9. _____	☐	☐
10. _____	☐	☐

For any of those people you have listed and indicated that you feel your relationship could be improved, what are you doing about it? Is there anything you can do about it? If you are willing to spend some time answering these questions, you will be a better and happier person because of it.

In some cases, what you do to change the way you relate to or communicate with that person might be minor. In other situations, it may be more involved and require more of an effort on your part. To help you put this thought into proper perspective, consider this:

How Would You Like Your Epitaph to Read?

If you're like most people, at one time or another in your lifetime you have been asked this question. What would you want engraved on your headstone? How do you want to be remembered? Then, of course, there is the more unsettling and unknown question, *"What would others say about me?"*

Before you make any major attempt to change the way you relate or communicate, I strongly encourage you to finish reading this book. As we connect, I hope you will develop a better sense of who you are, how important your method of communicating with others is, and what you can do to improve your relationships.

CHAPTER THREE

... *GET SET* ...

Setting the Stage for Improving Your Communication Skills!

Three truck drivers, made hard of hearing by years behind the wheel, met outside a café.

"Windy, isn't it?" remarked one of them.

"No, no," replied the second, "It's Thursday."

"So am I," declared the third. "Let's get a cup of coffee."

Sometimes you have to learn to work with what you've got!

Get Set

As I stated earlier, I believe with all my heart that *people can improve upon their patterns of communication if they want to.* Clearly, the key phrase here is *"if they want to."*

Improving communication skills should not be one of the most difficult things in life to accomplish. Changing communication skills can yield immediate and obvious rewards. You can see if new "techniques" you try are working with every verbal encounter you have.

Improving your communication skills does require effort and a true commitment on your part. If you are happy and satisfied with your current level of skills, then this book will have very little value for you. However, if you do want to improve the way you communicate on any or all levels, believe that you can. Trust me, I have personally experienced and witnessed positive communication changes and it can be done—*if you want to!*

So before we go any further, give this some serious thought: Do you really want to change and improve the way you communicate? Are you willing to put forth the effort that may be required?

OK. Have you thought about it? Have you decided that you do want to continue and to improve? All right, here goes!

After you have decided to make a serious effort at changing or improving, you now need to decide what areas of your communication skills you want to change. You may not need a complete makeover. There may be only certain areas of your communication techniques that you feel need fine-tuning. Do you feel a lack of confidence in social situations? Perhaps you think you could be doing better in your work environment. You should target areas for change. This isn't always easy. If you are having a problem deciding what it is that you want to improve upon, you might ask someone close to you for help. Try to choose someone who does not intimidate you and with whom you feel comfortable. Ask them if there is anything that they have ever noticed about you and the way you relate to and communicate with other people that might need improvement.

Asking someone this kind of question may be the most difficult thing you will do in order to become a better communicator and develop better relationships. As a way to open the conversation, you might ask that person if he/she has heard about my book. If so, then he/she may recognize what you're trying to do. If not, you could say, "I read this book on communication that I found utterly amazing and wonderful!" (Hey, can't blame a guy for trying!) "I was wondering if you would be willing to answer a couple of personal questions about me." Then you simply proceed with asking how he/she perceives your communication skills.

This person will become your mentor. Finding and establishing a mentor will be very important in this whole process. This is not to say that you cannot improve your ability to communicate without a mentor. However, I really believe that it will help you tremendously if you have some other person to work with you in this process. He/she can provide instant feedback about how you are developing and improving.

The other important thing to note here is that if you select a personal mentor, you are definitely making a commitment, which is a giant step on the road to success. It's like having someone to diet, study, or exercise with—it's easier with a "buddy."

There are some very basic rules that you need to share with your mentor and make clear before you begin:

1. Tell your mentor the area or areas of your communication skills you want to work on. Ask if he/she would help you observe how you communicate in these areas and how people respond to you. Be specific. For example, "I get the feeling people don't think I'm paying attention in conversations and I want to change that."

2. It is important to give your mentor the freedom to share with you any positive or negative feedback. He/she should be the kind of friend who would tell you—discreetly—when you had bad breath and know, in turn, that you won't be offended by mentioning it.

3. You may want to work out some key words or gestures that can be used when you make a "whoops" in your verbal exchanges.

4. It is important for you to set a time and date to review personal and social experiences that you have in common. This structured schedule conveys a feeling of seriousness and commitment.

5. Of course, it goes without saying that there must be confidentiality on the part of your mentor. You should also avoid the close friends who, while trying to be helpful, might take a mutual acquaintance aside to say something like, "Arnie thinks you think he doesn't listen very well." Good intentions won't help you improve your skills!

6. You may feel like offering this person something in exchange for working with you. Wouldn't it be a pleasant surprise if this special person wanted you to help him with his communication patterns in return?

Let me take a moment to share with you a personal experience regarding one of these "partnerships" that played a major role in my life.

Throughout my first year and a half of college, I did not have very good study habits and my grades showed it. At the same time, I began dating a very attractive, intelligent classmate of mine who was destined to become the love of my life. While I was keenly aware of her physical and inner beauty, I was also aware that she did not communicate well with others in some situations. She had a very honest and sincere manner when we were together, but lacked spontaneity and easy responsiveness in a variety of other social situations. During the initial stages of our courtship, we discussed her apprehensiveness and verbal discomfort. Some of my friends implied that she was "stuck-up," which was not true at all. She had the very same desire to be well liked as the rest of us; she simply didn't know what to say or how to respond.

During one of our many late-night discussions in my car (!), I suggested that we enter into a mutually beneficial contract. I may not have phrased it like that, but you get the idea. I proposed that if she would help me learn better study habits so I could improve my grades, I would help her with her interpersonal and social communication skills. Without hesitation, she agreed. With a handshake (or maybe it was a passionate kiss), we sealed the deal and it proved to be a very good deal for both of us.

I improved my grade point from a 1.6 to a 3.0 average, enough to be accepted into graduate school, and Betty—well, if you were to know Betty today, you would be surprised to know that she ever had any difficulty with communication skills. She is delightful company, a socially graceful conversationalist and as comfortable talking with clients, employees, and new acquaintances as she is with her own family. She is living proof of someone who made a significant and positive change in her interactive communication skills. Betty was able to make those changes because she wanted to, and also because she was willing to have me point out minor flaws and deficiencies that she had not identified. She is not the only person I know who made positive changes in communication skills, but she certainly is the one closest to me!

Something else you can do to improve your communication skills is to study positive communication techniques of others. Think about someone that you know and respect, and whom you admire for the way he/she communicates with others. Next, in a discreet way, observe how that person communicates with others. If you are with him/her in a variety of situations, so much the better because you can note many different forms of communication that work well for that person. Take special note of how he/she interacts with other people. Focus on one thing that person does while talking to others. It may not only be something that person says, but how it is said or the body language used.

As I have observed other people I admire, I take special note of how they greet people and how they answer simple questions such as "How are you?" I make mental notes about their posture, where they position themselves in a standing group of people, and what they do with their hands. I am always curious about how they say goodbye or how they gracefully move from one group of people to another.

The people I make a special effort to observe are always people who appear to me to have earned the respect and admiration of others. What sets them apart? Why do others seem comfortable talking to them? When I observe a special characteristic in someone else, I then try to determine if this is something that I can feel comfortable doing and add to my communications "repertoire." I am not advising you to precisely mimic someone else's mannerisms; however, it may help you to develop your version of a desirable personality characteristic.

If you have ever taken music lessons or been coached in athletics, it is obvious that your objective is to emulate or duplicate what your teacher or coach demonstrates for you. The better you are at honing those skills, the better you will become at whatever you are learning. In most cases, the coach or instructor has excelled in the area you are studying. The same principle exists when examining communication skills. You may not achieve the same skill level, but discipline and practice allow you to develop your own style while retaining the admirable qualities of your mentors. If you believe, as I do, that communication skills do impact your success in life, then you will agree that it is important to practice in your own mind those valuable mannerisms you observe and admire in others.

I would encourage you to do one more thing. It may not be critical to improving your communication skills, but it will do wonders for any relationship. At some time, tell the person you admire that you really like and appreciate the way he/she communicates and relates to other people and to you. Believe me, he/she will appreciate it, and it will make you feel good because you made someone else feel special.

Ask someone you admire to go out to lunch. On a number of occasions, I have called people whom I hold in high regard and asked them if I could treat them to lunch. I simply say I have admired their ability to achieve success (whether it be in business, family, community, social or other areas of their life), handle adversity, give a seminar, lead a committee, etc. It is never clear to me who enjoys this more, I or my guest. If someone called you out of the blue and asked to take you to lunch out of admiration for something special that you do in life, how would that make you feel? Try it. I guarantee you that you will enjoy it.

Put Your Broccoli Where Your Mouth Is

As I have said before and know I will say again, people *can* make positive changes in their lives *if they want to.* Since I firmly believe this and since I make that proclamation quite often to others, I decided one day to try an experiment and to "walk the walk." I asked myself "What is something I do not like or do not like to do?" After a few minutes, an image appeared in my head—broccoli! I shuddered. Everyone in my family knows I hate broccoli. I said to myself, if I could change the way I feel about broccoli, that would help confirm in my own mind that people can make positive changes if they want to.

I had to develop a plan. I decided to change the way I felt about broccoli, and I would do it one step at a time.

Wouldn't you know it, almost the next day, I found myself at a luncheon buffet with broccoli. (Incidentally, after starting this plan, I couldn't believe how many times the dreaded vegetable turned up in meals!)

To begin this process, I decided to take a very small portion and also to combine my bites of broccoli with something else. In other words, try to trick my mouth! It took awhile, but slowly I began to dislike broccoli less than I previously had (notice I didn't say "like" it—I just didn't *dislike* it as much!). Slowly but surely, I began to successfully integrate this dark green vegetable into my diet. It is still not my vegetable of choice, but I can honestly say that now I always take some broccoli when it is part of a meal. I can do so without holding my breath and actually like its crisp texture and refreshing taste. Can you believe it? I am so proud of myself, especially now when I read articles about how beneficial it is for us. It makes my mom happy to know that, finally, her son is eating right!

You may think this is a strange analogy and that it has nothing to do with improving your communication skills. But the point of the story is that since I was always telling others how they could change if they really wanted to, I had to have some graphic and measurable experiment to prove my point.

Two very important premises are part of this:
- I really wanted to change the way I felt. I hated broccoli but wanted to be able to eat it.
- I had to make a conscious effort to change. I had to learn to tolerate and maybe even like broccoli.

The same holds true if someone wants to improve his communication skills. You have to really want to change and improve the way you communicate with others, and you have to work at it. Believe me, it will be worth it.

Another benefit to learning to like broccoli is that I no longer have to listen to my family constantly telling me "You don't know what you're missing." And that's a silly statement if ever there was one—how can you miss something you choose not to eat and that makes you sick to your stomach at just the thought? Just don't ask me to extend my experiment to include cauliflower. There are limits! I have proven my point to myself and my family, and yes, I do know what I'm missing!

Another step to improving the way you communicate with others is one you've already taken—reading self-help books such as this one. This may seem obvious, but sometimes all of us need some encouragement to act upon even the most obvious suggestion. There are so many good books to select from these days. The publication of non-fiction books has been on a steady increase for years, and the self-help section continues to grow. It just proves that people continue to look for ways to help themselves improve in all areas of life—so you are not alone in your quest.

I often hear people say that they just don't have the time to read self-help books. It would be much more accurate if they would simply say that reading self-help books is not high enough on their list of priorities to include it in their lifestyle. I'm not saying such books should be on your daily reading list, but I always have some positive mental attitude book available so I can read it when time permits. I never seem to find the time to read any novels. Okay, I meant to say that reading novels is not high enough on my list of priorities to fit it into my schedule.

Finally, those individuals who aggressively want to improve their communication skills can enroll in classes such as Dale Carnegie, or organizations such as the Optimists or Toastmasters, which emphasize public speaking and positive thinking.

Over the past twenty-five years, I've purchased and read many self-help books. I could pick up any one of them and find some words or suggestions that have contributed significantly to the success in my business life and the fulfillment of my personal life. *You can too!*

CHAPTER FOUR

... AND GO! ...

Looking at the Key Aspects
of Effective Communication!

Two tourists were driving through Texas. As they approached the town of Nacogdoches, they started arguing about the pronunciation of the name of the town. They argued back and forth until they stopped for lunch.

As they stood at the counter of a fast food restaurant, one tourist asked the employee behind the counter, "Before we order, could you please settle an argument for us? Would you please pronounce where we are...very slowly so we can understand it?"

The employee smiled agreeably, leaned forward and said, "Burrrrrrr-gerrrrrrrrrrrrrrrrr------Kinnnnnnnngggg."

**You have to ask the right question if you
want the right answer!**

And Go!

When we think about improving relationships, we usually think about family or friends. In a true friendship, as well as between family members, we assume that the interest we have in each other is mutual. Very few friendships or close family relationships exist where interest is one-sided (although probably we all have a case of unrequited love from our teen-age years!).

So where do we begin to assess and improve our communication skills? With that most difficult and painful of tasks—self-examination. To get us started, let's take a look at a number of key aspects of communication and, as you read, be thinking of how they apply to you.

- F.O.R.M. A Sincere Interest
- Use A Name
- Say "HI" First
- Acknowledge Their Words
- Focus On Others
- Be Positive
- Treat Everyone With Respect
- Our Words Affect Other People

F.O.R.M. a Sincere Interest

If you want to become better liked and more accepted in social circles, make sure you demonstrate a sincere interest in people. I learned a long time ago, both in my personal and professional life, that there is nothing people would rather talk about than themselves. If you want to make a positive impression on others, ask them about themselves (and listen to their answers!).

In our Kitchen Solvers' business, we train new franchises how to make a positive connection with prospective customers by urging them to use what we call the **FORM Method**. We encourage them to ask questions about Family, Occupation, and Recreational interests, which results in a Message. This message about customers communicates who they are, what they like, and what is important to them. In asking these kinds of questions, the goal is to find a common bond—an area of interest or an experience that the salesperson and customer share. Our people begin to establish a very important link in the chain of exchanges that will take place between the two parties, a link that will, with luck and persistence, lead to a mutual interest. Oh yes, and a sale!

In the pursuit of being well-liked and accepted by others, I cannot impress upon you enough the importance of showing an interest in other people. If you want to increase your popularity and deepen your interpersonal relationships, remember the word **FORM**.

Let me illustrate the effectiveness of using the **FORM** method.

Several months ago Betty and I were dinner guests at a friend's house. During the evening, I mentioned that I was thinking of writing a book on communication skills. Dave Woggon, a business associate, confessed that in many social settings he is uncomfortable and becomes very quiet. To those of us around the table who know Dave, this came as a surprise since at work he is an outgoing and gregarious guy and people genuinely enjoy working with him.

I suggested that, on those occasions when he felt uncomfortable, Dave simply ask people questions about themselves, essentially using our **FORM** method of conversation.

Recently, he informed me that he had taken my suggestion seriously and it had been working! Not only did this incident reinforce my belief in using the **FORM** method, but it also underlined the fact that all of us have communication skills that are not as strong in one area (i.e., social) as they might be in another (work), and we all can work on those areas to improve our confidence and skill.

At one point during a recent conversation with Dave (while interviewing him for this book), he indicated that he considered me to be a good communicator. He said I spoke with confidence and was able to address a number of subjects during the course of my daily conversations. Pleased with the compliment, I realized how important it is for me to keep informed and up-to-date on a variety of topics.

Because I love to read, it is relatively easy to keep current on state, local and national politics, our economy, world events, business matters, religion, etc. But my interest pays off in more than just keeping me informed. It allows me to be able to contribute to almost any conversation and to speak knowledgably (and therefore, confidently) about a wide range of topics.

Examining this closer, I discovered yet another thing about myself: In general conversations, I intentionally ask people questions about topics which I know something. By doing so, I have accomplished two things. I have made the person I am talking to feel good because I have sought out his or her opinion and thoughts on a subject. Additionally, I have assured myself that I will have something to add to the discussion and can feel confident that I will be able to "hold up my end of the conversation." That is what they call a "win-win" situation!

Along the same line of asking people about themselves is seeking their opinion or advice. All people have opinions, and, oh, do we love to share them. Asking for an opinion on almost anything is saying, *"I value you enough to seek your opinion and feelings about this."* Just remember—do not *give* advice unless asked, and do not be offended if *your* advice is not taken. (At the risk of being labeled sexist: gentlemen, never, *never* offer an opinion, even when asked, if a woman says, "Does this outfit make me look fat?" There simply is no correct answer or opinion you can give to that question!)

It is relatively easy to make a positive impression on people by simply giving compliments or making special notice of something new. Say something nice about someone's hair, dress, tie, or the family. If you don't think comments like this "make points" with others, just think about it. Do you like it when someone notices you have a new suit? How do you feel when someone compliments your hairstyle? For those of you who are parents or grandparents, don't you feel a warm glow when someone makes a positive comment about your kids or grandchildren? I think everyone would answer "yes" to these questions.

You meet a friend on the street and she has a new hair style, hair color, a shirt, something that you know she knows you have noticed. She either asks for your opinion or expects you to comment on it. And all you can think to say is "What were you thinking?!?" How do you get yourself out of this gracefully? Avoid adjectives! It sounds silly, but it works. "Now *that* is a haircut!" you say enthusiastically. You need not say it looks as if a John Deere tractor worked its way across the head. "*That* is some kind of shirt, Harry!" No need to tell him it is the kind of shirt that should be used to grease the John Deere tractor! I have a friend who says this method of avoiding adjectives works wonders when friends show her pictures of their newborn children. She simply looks at the picture and croons "Ohhh, *what* a baby," and she doesn't have to admit that there was some doubt in her mind as to what kind of baby it was.

More than likely, most of you take the time and make the effort to show interest in others; however, there are a number of people who do not reciprocate by showing the same interest in you. My question to those people is "Why not?" That apparent disinterest usually translates into a perception of being self-centered or simply not caring. If this sounds like you, and if you truly aren't interested in other people, don't worry—I can assure you that you aren't going to have many people trying to talk to you after awhile anyway.

Don't like hearing that about yourself? Sorry. As a part of a routine "check-up from the neck up," a certain amount of constructive criticism is necessary. I hope that if my comments or suggestions hit home, you will work towards making some positive corrections in the way you communicate with others.

Steve Plopper, a good friend of mine for several years and an employee, shared an interesting analogy with me when I asked him how he felt about people who were non-reciprocal in conversation. He said talking to such people is like playing tennis with someone who never makes an effort to return the ball. The game is pretty boring and, more than likely, the opponent would not be someone you're going to call for another game.

For just a few minutes, I would like to have each of you reflect on your last social occasion and ask yourself these questions:
- Who did I enjoy visiting with the most and why?
- Did other people ask me more questions about myself than I asked them?
- Did others appear to enjoy visiting with me?
- Were most of my conversations dialogues, or did I turn them into monologues by dominating the conversation?

If you are someone who tends to dominate conversations, I encourage you to work towards creating more of a balance in your oral exchanges.

Something I discovered in my research interviews on communication was that most people find it difficult to communicate with those who either do not reciprocate or tend to monopolize the discussions, and both are unsettling. What is most important is that all people involved in a conversation feel as though they are making a contribution.

Use a Name

It has been said that the most important word anyone can hear is his or her own name. Think about it—do you like it when someone calls you by name? Of course you do! (A possible exception might be when a parent or spouse throws in your middle name—then you know you're in trouble!) Which brings me to my next suggestion. It is a simple one to implement, but extremely important in creating a positive impression. *Make sure that you try to use the name of the person to whom you are talking.* I don't mean saying his name in every other sentence. Simply use it as often as it seems appropriate in the course of conversation.

Of course, using a person's name requires that you first *remember* the name (there's always a catch, isn't there?). For some of us, that is easier said than done. Some people seem to maintain a mental file of index cards with faces and names; others of us have to create visual or memory hooks to help recall the name at a later date.

I said at first that using someone's name was a simple suggestion, but it gets more complicated. Not only do you have to remember the name, you should make certain you're pronouncing it correctly! My own personal experience will illustrate how important it is to be in a conversation where someone uses and pronounces your name correctly.

My name is spelled "Gerald." For the majority of people whose name is spelled like mine, the "G" has the soft "J" sound (as in "jelly"). However, when pronounced correctly, my given name uses a hard "G" (as in "gravy"). Just a brief history how this happened. When my mother was pregnant with me, she and my father thought they were going to have another daughter to join my four-year old sister. They had chosen a girl's name—*Carol*— but had not picked out a name for a boy. Never did they guess that they were having twins, and that one of them would be a boy! When my sister was born, they named her Carol, as planned. When I made my surprise appearance ten minutes later, they wanted to come up with a boy's name that sounded like Carol, so they chose *Gerald*, with a hard G. And so I received a name which has been a challenge for others all of my life.

Pronouncing my name correctly has been a problem for other people throughout my life. Even when I know they are making a concerted effort to say it correctly, I know it causes them difficulty. I can meet someone for the second or third time and tell they are struggling to remember how my name is pronounced.

After Betty and I had been married for about fifteen years, because of the frustration I was experiencing with my name and the necessity to explain its pronunciation all the time, we thought we would try a change. My hope was that others would then call me by the same name that Betty did. *Jerry* was to be my new name! We tried to make the change for about four weeks. But it seemed so foreign for her to call me "Jerry" after fifteen years of being Gerald, and I just didn't feel like a Jerry! We almost felt like we were having an illicit relationship! So the attempt failed and she once again called me by my given name.

Even in close interpersonal relationships, it is not only appropriate to use another's name in conversations, but strongly encouraged. Can you think of someone who uses your name frequently while you are talking? Do you remember how it makes you feel? It feels good, doesn't it? That, in turn, makes you feel good about that person.

As I think about people who use my name frequently during a conversation, it increases my respect for them, and, in most cases, they are respected by others. So try to remember people's names, use their names in conversations with them, and pronounce them correctly. Trust me, it will please them.

Simply cannot remember people's names, no matter how many times you meet them? I have a friend who is a wonderful guy—popular, outgoing, loves being with people and people love being around him—but he has a hard time remembering their names. So he doesn't try for their names—he calls everyone "Pal." Men and women alike are simply "Pal." "Hey, Pal, great to see you." How's everything been going, Pal?" No one seems too concerned that he can't remember their names because he is so sincere and enthusiastic when he meets them, making everyone feel important and welcomed. Regional customs are also acceptable—in the South and Southeast parts of the US, "darlin'" and "hon" are acceptable forms of affectionate address. Try out several names on your mentor and see which one might work and which one you can remember!

Say "Hi" First

Since we are talking about addressing people, I would like to share a little pet peeve of mine. It is frustrating to me when I feel as if I am always the first one to say "hi." And I have discovered that I am not alone in this dislike. Why should it always be one person's responsibility to say "hi" first?

If you're one of those who only feel it appropriate to "speak when spoken to," I'll have to ask you "why?" I am not talking about greeting someone that you have never met before; rather, I mean exchanging informal greetings with people that you already know and encounter during the day. In those kinds of exchanges, it always makes me wonder if that person thinks he/she is more important than I. If you're guilty of the "say-hi-second syndrome" and you do not want to give the impression of being arrogant or "better than thou," I strongly encourage you to be unselfish with your "hellos" and, of course, use people's names when you greet them.

So you've said hello first and called someone by name. Now what? Have you ever really thought about it? This would be a good time to use some of the FORM questions I mentioned earlier. Or maybe it's appropriate to say "How are you doing? or "How have you been?" Avoid the vague, open-ended questions such as "What do you know?" or "What's up?" When people ask those questions, is it really their intent to gain knowledge about me? Hardly. In fact, one major brewing company is well-known for its series of "Whassup?" commercials where friends greet each other with an exuberant "Whassup!" It is quite evident that no response is expected to this casual greeting. A later commercial in the series gently teases the country boy who, in response to a casual "How you doin'?" from Brooklyn bar patrons, launches into a genial, but lengthy, explanation of how he is doing, stunning his audience into silence.

But if you are not starring in one of these commercials, the vague "what's up" type of question usually serves only to make the other person feel uncomfortable. Asking "what do you know?" often implies that the person is expected to respond with something funny or clever, and it is usually difficult to respond spontaneously with a humorous answer.

Rehearse! If someone should ask you "What's up?" or "What do you know?" you might have one or two basic responses at hand like "Not much," or "No more today than yesterday." It is good to have some idea of what to say in those situations because the asker is probably going to wait for a response. Have one or two answers in mind and you'll amaze them with your instant wit!

Acknowledge Their Words

Another question for you. Have you ever been in a conversation with people who do not acknowledge what you have said by either agreeing or disagreeing? They simply stare blankly at you as if you were from another world. It is very frustrating, isn't it? When I am in a conversation with someone like that, I am always tempted to say, "Yoohoo, anybody home?"

If you want other people to enjoy visiting with you, make sure you give them verbal responses to acknowledge that you have heard what they said. Likewise, it is just as important to give them non-verbal gestures or cues, such as a nod or smile. Let them know you are interested in what they have to say. Believe me, they will be a lot more interested in what you say if they think it is a mutual exchange.

Focus on Others - Taking the "I" Test

Try to recall at least five of your recent interpersonal conversations and ask yourself this question: How often did I use the word "I"? Because it is important that you have a handle on whether or not you pass the "I" test, I want you to really think about this. Try to recall when you have been in a conversation with someone who acted as if no one else existed in the world except him. There are people I try to avoid in social situations because their conversations are always about *me, myself and I.*

How do you avoid being a conversation hog? It goes back to our FORM questions. Most people enjoy being in the presence of a good listener. Ask them questions and *listen* for the answers. Listen for feelings and emotions that people attach to their words. Do they say "I'm fine" with sarcasm? Sadness? Enthusiasm? It is easier for you to respond appropriately, and with interest, if you train yourself to pick up on the verbal clues people drop.

A physical means of focusing on people is to make good eye contact. For some people, this is easy to do; for others, it takes an effort. However, I can assure you that the kind of eye contact you make with others leaves a lasting and important impression. One friend of mine complains that a mutual acquaintance of ours is always looking over her shoulder. *"He's talking to me, but all the time he's checking out everyone else in the room. It's like saying 'someone more interesting might come in and I want to be ready to leave here if they do.' It sure doesn't make me feel good."*

It has been said often that people who can't (or won't) make eye contact cannot be trusted. This may or may not be true, but why take a chance on people not trusting you because you cannot look them in the eye?

Having trouble meeting people's gazes and maintaining eye contact while talking with them? Try looking directly at the spot *between* their eyes, just above the bridge of the nose. To them, it will look as though you are looking them right in the eyes!

Be Positive

This is not a book specifically written about how to develop a positive attitude (there are plenty on the shelves already and I encourage you to read one or two). Rather, as part of your mission to develop better relationships, I recommend that you make every effort to project a positive attitude towards others. The antithesis of this is to be pessimistic and negative.

Answer this simple question: Would you rather be around someone who has a positive outlook on life, someone who makes the proverbial lemonade out of life's lemons, or would you prefer to be in the company of someone who is constantly looking for the worst to happen? Examine your own attitude— are you running around expecting bad things to happen, raining on other people's parades, and having a generally negative outlook on life? *Stop it this minute!!* There are several reasons why you should work towards developing a positive attitude.

First, being negative around others really makes them feel bad. Let's say you and several other colleagues are in a business meeting. Harry makes a suggestion that might save the company some money, but all you can think of is why implementing that program would be too hard and probably not work. What has your negative attitude done? The idea you just rained on may have been very important to Harry. By pointing out all the negatives, you are telling Harry, essentially, that he isn't very good at something, and that his ideas are without value.

The second reason for not being a pessimist is because it discourages other people from sharing future thoughts and ideas with you. If you make a career out of always looking to see why something *won't* work, you will soon find yourself with a reputation for being a defeatist. If Harry's plan happens to have some flaws, look first for the positive aspects of the plan and build on those before mentioning the flaws.

There is a growing body of research that gives the best reason for having a positive attitude. You'll live longer and be healthier! Many scientific studies now show that people who have positive attitudes and surround themselves with positive thinkers can weather the trials and tribulations of life better, have fewer illnesses, and recover more quickly from disease. If that doesn't make you want to have a positive attitude in life, I don't know what will.

Treat Everyone with Respect

There's an old saying that it's a good idea to be nice to everyone on the way up the ladder of success because you never know if you may meet them on your way down! The same goes for communication. It is very important that you communicate to all people in the same way. Project a friendly attitude towards everyone you meet and work with on a daily basis, regardless of social status. Not only is it the right thing to do, it can also pay positive dividends in the future.

Our Words Affect Other People

Some years back, while a social worker in a small rural elementary school in Iowa, I was able to observe first-hand how much emotion is attached to the words we use with others. It appeared that a group of approximately 75 sixth graders had a higher degree of tension, conflict and rivalry than normal. Both the teachers and the principal felt that the "put downs," the maneuvers of cliques, and the frequent criticism of peers were destructive factors within the classroom and not conducive to a positive learning atmosphere.

Working with the school principal and the four teachers involved, I set out to study the situation and attempt to implement a behavior modification program to address the problem.

We first determined that it was necessary to specifically identify the problem areas. Even though several different instances were related, eventually these situations were reduced to a common denominator, and it was agreed that what was being discussed involved the "feelings" that occurred among students. They appeared to be insensitive to the feelings of their peers. Hurt and angry feelings, a result of discourteous and thoughtless remarks made to classmates, were readily observed by the teachers. Even though insensitivity to others' feelings and discourteous remarks tend to be typical of sixth grade behavior, the high incidence appeared to be somewhat abnormal. Teachers were frustrated by the destructive atmosphere that their students were promoting and were concerned about how to deal with the situation. It was difficult for teachers not to be drawn into the crossfire and they resented the amount of time being devoted to countering this destructive force.

At this point, it seemed necessary to assess student attitudes in regard to their relationships with classmates. Thus, during the following week, the principal gave each student a questionnaire. Even though the purpose was to discover student attitudes towards peer interaction, this was camouflaged with questions dealing with other subjects as well. After the results were tabulated and evaluated, it was concluded that students were definitely aware of intense feelings and rivalry.

We had defined the problem. Now what? Different methods of dealing with this inappropriate behavior were discussed; however, nothing seemed appropriate until the discussion touched upon the theory of Transactional Analysis— essentially, the interactions that occur among people. As the discussion of TA and its philosophy/practice continued, we tried to think of ways it could be applied within the classroom to address our problem.

One of the basic concepts within the total TA theory is that as human beings, we stroke each other's feelings by and through our interaction with the people we meet. These strokes are classified as either positive or negative, depending upon how they are received, regardless of how they are meant. In TA terminology, these strokes are called "warm fuzzies" (positive) and "cold pricklies" (negative). I designed a program to help students become aware of the warm fuzzy and cold prickly feelings they were receiving and sending.

It was assumed that it was difficult, awkward and embarrassing for the students to know how to react or respond to either positive or negative feelings. Using this assumption as the hypothesis guiding the program, I decided that the warm fuzzy and cold prickly terminology would be used in implementing a program to help students identify and deal with their feelings. Students were asked to wear two tags—one for warm fuzzies and one for cold pricklies. The purpose of each student wearing both tags was to help them identify positive and negative feelings. Students were then told that when someone gave them a positive or negative feeling, they were to put a mark on that student's corresponding tag. In other words, when Jane told Sally she liked her sweater, Sally would put a mark on Jane's positive tag. It was felt that this non-verbal evaluation would not only be a less threatening way of dealing with feelings, but would also help them become more aware and sensitive as to how their responses and behaviors were being received by others. The necessity of imposing a time limit on this exercise was important, so we made ours two weeks.

Teachers were given the option of wearing tags. All four agreed that it would be important to the success of the program to be included just like the students. It was agreed, however, that marking students' tags would not be used in any form of discipline.

We were ready to begin. The following Monday morning, I spent an hour in each of the three classrooms, explaining the program and talking about positive and negative feelings and what effect, if any, these feelings have on us. There appeared to be consensus within the groups that there had been a lot of putdowns recently, and that the rivalry, criticism and competitiveness had been quite evident. Students were then asked to identify those feelings that could be categorized as positive or negative. The responses were numerous and represented a broad spectrum. Main ones were:

POSITIVE		NEGATIVE	
Accepted	Friendly	Angry	Disappointed
Glad	Happy	Lonely	Disliked
Joyous	Loved	Dumb	Mad
Wanted		Sad	Put down
		Unfriendly	Embarrassed
		Hate	Unloved
		Hurt	Unneeded
		Ignored	Unwanted

As is evident, students thought of many more negative feelings than positive feelings.

It was then explained to students how they could deal with these feelings. At the beginning of each day, every student would receive a tag to wear. Should someone give them either a good feeling or a bad feeling, they were to mark that person's corresponding tag. Teachers were asked to record their feelings each day about how they felt the program was progressing. Each one felt that the first day of the program had created a lot of tension and additional responsibilities for them; however, as the week and program continued, attitudes towards both the program and the functioning of the program itself seemed to improve a great deal.

At the end of the first week, tabulations indicated that the warm fuzzies outnumbered the cold pricklies by almost five to one. It came as a surprise because a greater number of negative feelings were being described by the students than positive ones.

As the second week started, I helped the students evaluate their experience of the week before. Students felt that the program had been quite effective in school and several indicated that it prompted them to discuss feelings within their own families. Some students informed the class that they continued to identify warm fuzzies and cold pricklies at home, and that it made it easier for them to deal with their feelings. Teachers indicated they had seen a tremendous change in some of the students who previously had been very active in issuing criticism and putdowns.

Students indicated that it was difficult and awkward for them to mark their teachers' tags. Consequently, teachers did not have as many marks as we had hoped for. However, it could be assumed that this is typical and perhaps indicative of the respect and/or fear students have regarding teachers as authority figures.

To me, this exercise was a perfect example of the powerful effect our words have on others. Even though kids at the age of 12 and 13 are not generally as sensitive to feelings as most people are when they become adults, we should not underestimate the impact our words have on other people, intentional or not.

Communicate Your Way Through Conflict

It is doubtful that any of us can go through a day without observing or experiencing conflict. It affects our personal sense of well-being, and taken to the extreme, can negatively influence entire work environments, social settings, or family relationships. As I said in an earlier chapter, I try to avoid conflict *whenever possible,* but when it is not possible, I seek a resolution that is acceptable for all parties involved as quickly as I can.

Let's look at how to deal with personal conflict between two people, whether family members, friends or colleagues. I have heard some people say that the best way to deal with conflict is to just forget about it and the negative or hurt feelings will go away. That may work if the conflict is minor. If the hurt feelings are small, or if the person who offended you or whom you offended is someone you seldom see, it may be appropriate to deal with it in this way. Every relationship we have does not need to be a meaningful one. However, most personal conflicts take place between people for whom the prospect of continuing a meaningful relationship *is* important. I have seen family relationships literally destroyed because family members could not communicate about or resolve their differences.

Taking that into consideration, let's look at the following analogy: You're pulling weeds in your garden, but it is dry and difficult to get at the roots. You struggle, but end up with just the leaves that grew above ground. What happens to the weed? A week or two later, it's back! That's the way it is with conflict or hurt feelings. If you do not deal with them appropriately, they will eventually raise their ugly heads and come to the surface again. It is extremely important to deal with the "root" of the problem.

Maybe the person who hurt your feelings was never aware that what was said caused you mental stress or pain; maybe you were unaware of hurting someone else's feelings. It is hard to address and correct a slight or a misunderstanding if you do not know it exists.

It has always been important in my family to get things out in the open. If I have said or done anything that upset someone else, I want to know so that we can talk it through and wipe the slate clean. I believe that strong and meaningful relationships are built on honesty and open communication.

Have you ever heard anyone who is any kind of authority on communication and counseling suggest that the best way to deal with conflict in relationships is *not* to talk about it? I don't think so.

Is it easy to discuss conflict with someone you care about and someone who cares about you? Of course not. It just depends on how much you are willing to invest in a relationship with someone. You must be committed to working things out (or at least trying) before you approach the person involved with your concern.

Many years ago, it became increasingly clear that some tension and negative feelings were erupting between my older sister and me. It really began to bother me, and I was certain that it weighed heavily on her mind as well. (Ask me now and I couldn't tell you what the specific issues were!) I felt that the only way these negative feelings would go away for both of us was to talk about them and address them openly. Even though it was difficult, I finally mustered up the nerve to dial the number (for you young folks who don't know what "dial a number" means, please talk to your parents!). My suggestion to get together and talk was accepted, and we agreed to meet halfway at a restaurant—neutral ground, if you will.

Without going into a lot of details (mainly because I cannot recall the actual words and issues), it turned out to be a very positive exchange. We each respectfully expressed our feelings and discovered that we both had misinterpreted things said or done in the past. The one thing I do recall clearly was the feeling of almost exhilaration when we hugged goodbye. For me, it was the proverbial huge weight off my shoulders. It was communication at its best. And I knew my sister felt the same way. If we both had not taken the risk of communicating our feelings to each other, those emotions and "cold pricklies" would have continued to grow and would have severely damaged what had been—and is once again—a relationship of love and respect.

It is important to note here that in order for this form of clarifying communication to have positive results, it is essential that several very important factors be in place:

- Both parties are willing to invest some time and effort into resolving the conflict;
- Each party is willing to take the risk of communicating innermost feelings regarding the situation;
- Each person is able to share concerns in a non-hostile and non-aggressive (calm) voice;
- Each party is willing to apologize and sincerely say "I'm sorry" for anything that might have been said to cause hurt feelings.

By the way, saying "I'm sorry," is not easy, but it's essential, and worth discussing in its own chapter!

Lindy Saline, a friend of mine and a former top executive for General Electric, shared with me his philosophy on how to resolve conflict through good communication strategies. First of all, he says that it is essential for all parties involved to understand just what the basis of conflict is. Each person must understand how the other feels about what caused the conflict.

Secondly, it must be established from the outset the degree of trust that exists between all parties involved. In some cases, if there is no comfortable mutual level of trust, it may be necessary to openly discuss *that* situation before seeking any conflict resolution. That may involve openly asking the person if mutual trust exists, and what, if anything, has been done to jeopardize that trust. Thirdly, each party should offer or suggest what can be done to alleviate the conflict. Finally, it is important for all parties involved to understand what their personal and emotional reward for resolving past differences will be.

Who Do You Think You Are?

A long time ago, I read a very interesting commentary regarding who we think we are. The writer quite cleverly made the premise that who we think we are has several answers and there are really several versions of ourselves.

1. *The person that you really are* - It is very possible that you have not yet fully discovered the person you really are. In some ways, life is an endless journey of trying to find the answer to this question. That you may not have fully discovered who you are is not necessarily a bad thing. It can be very consequential for everyone to learn something new about themselves on a continuing basis and to discover what is important to them. Have you heard the phrase *"What you see is what you get"*? It might describe this person.

2. *The person that you think you are* - This would represent how you see yourself today. You would carefully choose the words to describe this person. I strongly suspect that very few people take time to

concentrate on this question. I think Phil McGraw in his book *Self Matters* does an excellent job of focusing on this issue. He encourages people to look into their past to help them better understand how events and experiences during different periods in their lives have contributed to who they are.

3. *The person others think you are* - This is the person your friends would describe when asked about you. How would your friends or family members describe you to a stranger? What nouns, pronouns, verbs, adverbs, etc. would they use? Are you curious? Good! I've often wanted to be a mouse in the corner when people are talking about me. I like to think I'd hear nothing but good things, but if I did hear something negative, I would take the steps to correct it.

4. *The person that you think others think you are* - Ideally, the answer to this statement would be the same as the answer to Question #1. However, in more cases than not, this isn't true. It could be important for you to strive to make the answers to #1 and #4 the same. Making sure that you have open and honest communication in your relationships would go a long way to achieving that goal.

5. *The person that you would really like to be* - This book is very closely related to this statement. I personally believe that every human being should have a never-ending goal of trying to improve himself. I don't care how old you are, it is never too late to improve upon the present model of yourself. Have you ever heard someone say about someone else, "He seems comfortable with who he is"? To me, that statement summarizes this characterization. I think all of us would like to be comfortable with who we are.

6. *The person that you think others want you to be* - This
thought truly exists within each of us, and it is this
aspect that quite often contributes to interpersonal
conflicts. That is not to say that other people should
not have their own expectations of who they would
like us to be; however, unless the person that they
want us to be and the person we want to become are
similar, it can serve as the basis of conflict between
us. If you are trying to change someone who does
not want to change, you are heading down a dead-
end road. People can only change when they want to.

More than likely, how similar the answers to all of these
questions are has a lot to say about how positive your self-image
and self-confidence are. If the answers to all of these questions
are very similar, you probably have an excellent self-image. All
of us strive toward continuity in the responses to these
questions. Of course, we cannot be sure about the answers that
involve others, but we probably have a pretty good idea.
Attempting to answer these six questions can be an interesting
exercise for you, one that you might consider reviewing every
six months or so.

Before I bring this chapter to a close, I would like to share a
personal discovery of mine. It is obvious that our failure to
communicate certain pieces of information or words of
affirmation at the appropriate times can cause problems. But it
is not always the spoken words that can cause relational
problems. Equally important are the words that are not heard
or spoken.

Over the past several years, I have developed a hearing loss. Consequently, I am now benefiting from the use of hearing aids. However, there are still those times when I do not hear certain words or phrases, and it can be a challenge for me and my family. This usually occurs between Betty and me, but because of the good communication pattern that we have developed over the years, we usually determine—sooner or later—that I did not hear something, and if it caused a problem it is resolved. This personally highlights for me the damage that can be done between two people, not necessarily because of words not heard but because of words not spoken. Once again, successful communication makes all the difference!

CHAPTER FIVE

WHAT DO YOU MEAN, "I DO"?

Communicating with Your Spouse

One day an old farmer walked into his lawyer's office and announced that he wanted a divorce. The young attorney was surprised.

"Henry, you've been married 46 years and you say you want a divorce now. Do you have any grounds?"

"Yep, I got about 40 acres."

"No, you don't understand. Do you have a case?"

"Nope. Been a John Deere man all my life."

"Henry, you don't understand," sighed the attorney. "Do you have a grudge?"

"Yep. That's where I keep my John Deere."

"No, Henry, do you think you have a suit?"

"Sure do. Wear it to church every Sunday."

The exasperated attorney shook his head.

"Henry, does your wife beat you up?"

"No sirree, we're both up by 5:00 every morning."

Finally the attorney said, "Okay, Henry, let me put it this way. Why do you want a divorce?"

"Well, after all these years, we just don't seem to be able to communicate."

Sound familiar?!?

What Do You Mean, "I Do?"

This is an interesting and enjoyable chapter for me. I have some pretty strong feelings about how communications contribute to or hinder a successful marriage. As I indicated in the introduction, Betty and I have been married for 38 years, and prior to my father's death in October 2001, my parents had been married for 63 years. Both of these marriages are very positive relationships between individuals who hold a lot of love and respect for each other. Does that mean that we never have conflicts or differences? Absolutely not! What it does mean is that we have figured out how to effectively resolve those disagreements.

Perhaps one of the most important things that any married couple can do is to determine effective ways of dealing with conflicts and resolving those issues without letting them grow and fester. It is impossible for two people to live under the same roof together without having some conflicts. You share the same bed, eat at the same table, share the same bathroom, spend each other's money, contribute dirty clothes to the laundry, have different sexual expectations, raise children together, have two sets of in-laws, etc. How could you possibly not have any conflicts? I once heard someone say that if a couple says they never have any disagreements between themselves, one of them is not necessary in that relationship. In other words, one person in a relationship such as that is always giving in to the other and keeping his/her feelings bottled up.

If you are reading this book and are married, or not married but you have a significant other, I would strongly suggest that you encourage that person to read this chapter as well, regardless of whether you think you have a communication problem or not. When we talk about communicating with a spouse, there's always room for improvement!

Before I discuss the importance of communication in a marriage, let's talk about the importance of communication *before* marriage. The level of communication that takes place during the dating and courtship stage of a relationship will, to a large degree, determine the kind of relationship you will have after you say "I do." Most people agree that it is passion that attracts us to one another. That is the fuel that keeps our fire going when we enter into courtship. But there is no doubt in my mind that it is *com*passion and compatibility that keep us attracted to each other after we are married. And, of course, it is the kind of commitment that we make to each other once we decide to tie the knot that helps us get through the difficult and challenging times that all married couples experience. Putting aside the infatuation that two people feel for each other, it is the communication between those two people about likes and dislikes, interests, hobbies and passions that will serve as the anchor to their marriage ship.

It is so important for prospective married couples to share and discuss such things as their desire to have children (and how many), personal hopes and dreams for their individual lives as well as for the life they will share together, religious beliefs, the kind of relationships they have (or hope to have) with immediate and extended families, interest in sports (or lack of it!), where they would like to live, their appetite for sexual intimacy, the amount of time they like to spend with friends, the need and desire for personal and private time, and the list goes on and on. It has been my personal and professional observation that couples who determine their compatibility in these critical areas of their lives prior to marriage tend to experience the most success and satisfaction in their married lives. It has also been my observation that couples who experience difficulty (and in many cases divorce) did not "do their homework" about their level or degree of compatibility prior to getting married.

Sometimes one of the individuals in the marriage did, in fact, exhibit compatibility prior to getting married, but after spending time together as a married couple, simply no longer had the same interest. Say, for example, a woman tells her family-loving boyfriend that she wants to have lots of children. He's delighted as he envisions three or four children filling the house. Then the suitcases are scarcely unpacked from the honeymoon before she declares she's gotten a promotion at work and no longer has any intention of having a family. This is devastating to the spouse who realizes there was a "bait and switch" phenomena present. Whether a courtship is long or short, it is absolutely essential that two people who are considering making a life-long commitment to each other discuss openly and honestly their interests and desires for the lives they want to lead following marriage.

Fortunately for Betty and me, we did discuss all of these issues during our two-year courtship. In fact, we very much enjoyed doing so. This is not to say that we agreed on every topic. Speaking for myself, I think I consciously made a mental checklist of those areas in which we agreed and those areas in which we did not share the same feeling. When you do that, it is obviously important to determine that you have more similarities than not.

Now let's talk about the communication with your spouse. It is more than likely that the relationship you have with your spouse is the most important relationship you have. How well you communicate with each other usually determines how happy you are in your marriage. I really believe that everyone who exchanges vows truly means it when they say "until death do us part." So what happens along the way that contributes to the tragically high (50%) percentage of those marriages that end in divorce? In too many cases, it is a breakdown in communication.

You have probably read many articles and books on marriage, so my thoughts may or may not be something you have heard before. However, the fact that you have chosen to read this book indicates that you do understand the important role that communication plays in your life, and perhaps I may raise an issue or two that you will consider closely.

Let me take a slight detour here while I share a little philosophy with you and use a business format to illustrate.

As I mentioned earlier, after Betty and I established a successful retail business (Kitchen Solvers), we decided to use the vehicle of franchising to expand what we considered to be a repeatable business concept. When we sell a franchise to people, and then train them, we strongly encourage (to the point of insistence) that they follow the system. We always say that if you want to be successful in your business, follow the guidelines for what has already proven to be successful. That is the premise that serves as the impetus for selling franchises and developing successful businesses for these individuals. I am fully aware that individuals bring their own unique set of personality characteristics to the table that will make it impossible to precisely mirror what our retail business looks like; however, we also know that if they follow the basic guidelines that we have laid out, they *will* be successful.

In part, this philosophy served as a contributing factor for me to write this book. I have seen first hand how following a proven successful system can lead to success for others. Using this scenario and this philosophy, I'll share with you what has proven to be a successful system in my own marriage. I do not believe that good marriages just happen. I believe good marriages evolve because two people have committed to each other to make it happen.

Many of the thoughts I will share may be obvious to you; on the other hand, I'd rather not assume anything. Someone once said that people who *"assume"* they know exactly what is going on make an ASS out of U and ME. !!!!

As I discuss the topic of communication with your spouse, I'll try to show you the significance of using all our God-given senses—sound, touch, sight and smell—to enhance the communication process.

It should go without saying (but I'll say it anyway) that above all else, we must be respectful of one another. In our similarities and especially in our differences, we must respect each other's feelings.

Perhaps the greatest strength of our marriage is that Betty and I do a very good job of communicating our feelings to each other. It is so important that your mate/spouse understands how you feel, regardless of the topic. Of course, there will be some topics that are more emotional by nature than others. Religious belief definitely is a more emotionally-charged topic than breakfast cereal preferences. Child-rearing philosophies will push more buttons than vacation destinations. It is important to pay attention to what the conversation means to each other. Something that may or may not have a lot of meaning to you may be very important to your spouse.

Fellas, let's say you love your wife's eyes, and so you tell her so. You're less enthralled with her habit of cracking her knuckles, but less likely to say anything. Yet it is equally as important to share those issues that you don't particularly care for as it is to remark on those areas that you like. You should always acknowledge things that your spouse says or does that make you feel good, feel proud, or that please you. It is very important to reinforce those traits. It makes her feel good about herself and the better she feels, the better she will (hopefully) feel about you. This should be a never-ending part of your marriage. Whenever possible, tell your soul mate that you are proud of him/her. Try very hard to build each other up instead of tearing each other down.

A short time ago Betty and I experienced a "bump in the road" and I suggested that we take time to think about the ten most desirable characteristics that we saw in each other. We wrote them down and later shared them with each other. It was a very positive experience at a time in our lives when we most needed it. It made us aware once again of why we valued each other and, most importantly, our marriage. It reminded us of the immeasurable good times we've shared and why it was worth working through the difficult times.

So always try to make a point of letting your spouse know what you like about her. It really isn't all that difficult. After all, there had to be a lot of things that attracted you in the first place and made you want to get married. Share some of these things on a continual basis.

Uncertain or uncomfortable about how to be complimentary to your spouse? Think of it as a first date. What would you say to the stranger across the table to let him/her know you're interested?

If you haven't shared something that you like about your spouse with him/her recently, then DO IT TODAY! Make a mental note of how your words are received. Was your spouse pleased? Surprised? Wondering who had kidnapped her real husband? Here are some examples of just a few of the countless ways we can compliment our spouse in daily life:

- I like the way that outfit looks on you.
- I appreciate you cleaning the recycle bin.
- That perfume certainly smells good on you.
- You handled that situation with our son/daughter very well.
- I appreciate your thoughtfulness toward me and others.
- That was a wonderful meal.
- You do a nice job of taking care of the lawn.
- I love waking up with you each morning.
- I appreciate how hard you work and the effort you put forth.
- I love you for who you are.

You get the idea.

Now let's move on to the importance of making your spouse aware of things you do not like or the unique idiosyncrasies that upset you. While it is important that you share this information, *how* you share it is critical.

Earlier I suggested that sometimes it is valuable to preface a thought or suggestion with sensitive words. This is one of those times. However, this is not the time to haul out the proverbial laundry list of petty gripes. And always remember, if you want to get the best results in trying to eliminate or change negative behavior, the best time to share these emotion-packed pieces of information is when you are not upset with each other.

I recall a counseling session I once had with a husband and wife who demonstrated numerous signs that they were having communication problems. (If you were to poll marriage counselors, you would find that most marital problems do not escalate necessarily because of the issues or conflicts themselves, but because those concerns were not communicated properly.) A conflict in and of itself indicates there are two or more people who do not share the same beliefs or attitudes about a certain topic. If there is either no communication or poor communication about those areas of disagreement, the conflict simply cannot be resolved.

Back to my married couple. In one of our sessions, I asked each of them to think about something they did not like about the other person. With very little hesitation, the husband said, "It really upsets me that you never make the bed." This couple had been married for fifteen years, and for all those years, every day started out on a negative note for him. Yet he had never told her. It completely bugged him and yet he had never mentioned it to her. What was simply her unconcern about making the bed grew to be perceived by him as a personal affront, something she was doing specifically to annoy him.

At their next counseling session, the husband came into my office with a slight grin on his face and could hardly wait to tell me how efficient his wife had become at bed-making! She heard what he had said and made what she considered to be the necessary adjustment. What is important here is not how they resolved the conflict, but rather that they communicated about this relatively insignificant behavioral pattern that was, for whatever reason, on the top of his mind. Yes, being bugged about an unmade bed probably is not a critical issue, but it got them started talking and sharing—baby steps, maybe, but steps forward.

The ongoing marriage counseling experience with this couple had a happy ending. However, I found that I literally had to coach them on how to communicate with each other. The significant ingredient in this positive experience was that they both wanted to improve the way they felt about each other.

Therefore, if there is something that "bugs" you about your spouse, I encourage you to share that feeling in a respectful and sensitive way. Don't always expect an immediate remedy to the problem. Often, it can take time for someone to change negative behavior patterns. And of course, when you do see positive change or even an effort to change negative behavior, make sure you let them know that you appreciate the effort. Above all else, whether you are the "bugger" or the "buggee," always remember that it is the behavior being criticized, not the person!

Oh, and just in case anyone is interested, Betty and I have been making the bed together in the morning for 38 years!! Now if she could just get me to put the cap back on the toothpaste tube!

Since I just referred to my counseling experiences, I want to share with you how important I believe counseling is for couples who are experiencing marital discord. It is very helpful to have someone with an objective viewpoint take a look through a magnifying glass at the intricacies of their relationship. Here again, it is essential that both individuals have a sincere desire to improve their relationship.

If you should decide that counseling may be appropriate for you, it's also critical that you both are comfortable with the counselor. An office and a title doesn't necessarily mean that this is the professional with whom you are going to share the intimate details of your life. During your first session, you are interviewing him. Make sure this is a person both of you feel comfortable with and one whom you think you can trust and respect.

Just to let you know how strongly I feel about the benefits of counseling, recently Betty and I went to a marriage counselor (yes, after 38 years of marriage) to help us fine tune our relationship. We had been experiencing some severe challenges within the family that caused us a great deal of stress, and some of that stress was spilling over into our relationship. In our case, we did not choose the first counselor we went to. The credentials were there, the experience was there, and yet we simply were not comfortable sharing our concerns with him. Fortunately, our second attempt found us a wonderful counselor, someone who was very sensitive and intuitive. Both of us developed an immediate sense of trust and respect for him as he guided us through our "38-Year Tune-Up." When choosing a counselor, choose someone you think you could be friends with, someone who does not intimidate you or make you feel uncomfortable. If it takes three or four tries, that's all right. This is too big an investment of your time and emotion to make the wrong choice.

Even though I know that for some people the financial cost of going to a marriage counselor may be a deterrent, I highly recommend that you not allow the cost to be a reason for not going. A quick look at some of the things we spend money on, things not nearly as important as our marriage, tells us that this money is well-spent. Check with local referral agencies—often such services are made available on an "ability to pay" basis. Clergy also are often available for family counseling. It has often been said that the best gift you can ever give your children is a good marriage. I'll take it a step further—it's the best gift you can give yourself and the person you love.

Let's look at another aspect that is very important to a good marriage, and that is the necessity of continuing to court your spouse. By this, I mean that even in the midst of a long-term marriage, it is still important to have those special times when you "date" each other.

Betty and I have always relished our "dates" together. Even when the children were young, we would hire a babysitter one night a month and go out to eat or a movie, just the two of us. We would dress up for each other, making every attempt to wear something we knew the other person liked. While we didn't prohibit "family talk," we made an effort to talk about things outside the family that were important to us. To this day, those special nights out are important to our marriage. Just making the effort to carry on with this tradition says to each other "I care about you and love you enough that I just want to be together with you and no one else."

I have heard parents say they never use a baby-sitter. If that means they are fortunate enough to have family or friends willing to watch the children on occasion, that's one thing. However, if it means that the two of them never go out by themselves, I think it is wrong, and it is certainly not doing the child any favors because this is a marriage that may be challenged. Such a couple is neglecting their marriage relationship when they should be nurturing it.

In keeping with the idea of nurturing the husband/wife relationship in order to strengthen the entire family relationship,

I would like to bring in another concern. At the risk of being labeled "shallow" or "superficial," I strongly encourage you always to make the effort to look good for your spouse. Now before anyone starts writing me letters, let me explain.

It was disheartening how many times while I was a marriage counselor I heard the phrase "He/she just let himself/herself go." The unspoken yet clearly communicated message was, *"The courtship is over and I have better things to do."* The effort you make to look attractive to your spouse says you still care. It communicates to your significant other that you value the relationship enough to work at it, and it nurtures that physical attraction that was part of your initial relationship.

Granted, there are any number of other factors that contribute to divorce, and not caring about one's appearance is probably symptomatic of a larger disease, but it is one that will kill a relationship if ignored.

Now let's talk about one of the most sensitive and taboo subjects in a relationship. No, not sex. Let's talk money!

Financial challenges or problems are significant factors in marriage problems. In a good marriage, both the husband and wife jointly make decisions that involve the earning, spending and budgeting of their money. You need to communicate to each other where your money is going and how it is to be spent. You both should be acutely aware of what your sources of income are and then budget accordingly. Unfortunately, I have seen too many marriages end up in divorce when debt, either individual or collective, has exceeded income.

For the first twenty years of our marriage, Betty and I operated on a monthly budget. We both knew exactly what our monthly income was and what all of our expenses were. There were never any surprises to either of us. If you want to get on the highway to divorce court, one sure way is to keep somebody in the dark about your over-spending habits, or to be in the dark about household expenses. The husband or wife who does not assume equal responsibility in financial matters contributes to the demise of a marriage. Communicate, communicate and then communicate some more about your finances!

A close relative of financial communication is the way in which you communicate your hopes and dreams to each other. For most people, realization of hopes and dreams are the end result of how well they handle their finances. It is very important to share with one another what your goals are for the future. If your dream vacation is a trip to Disneyworld, then you should discuss how to save for the trip. If you think that a brand new SUV would look good in your garage, then you need to look at your finances and see how it can be arranged. If going back to school and getting a degree so you can teach seems like the most fulfilling goal you can have, then the two of you need to sit down and see how you can best make it happen.

Successful corporations, small businesses, churches, even non-profit agencies, spend a great deal of time and resources on what is called "strategic long-term planning." It goes by other names, but what it boils down to is having a clear understanding of what the organization wants to accomplish in future years and how goals can be achieved. It helps focus all employees on common goals while building on shared resources and experiences. The same theory applies to marriage. Those times in our marriage when Betty and I collectively worked toward achieving some goal have served as very important building blocks in a mutually loving and respectful relationship.

When was the last time you sat down with your spouse over dinner or took a long walk in the park and talked about what you would like your life to look like five, ten, fifteen or twenty years from now? Communicate your personal aspirations as well as your goals as a couple and then (I know you have heard this before, but I'm going to tell you once again) WRITE THEM DOWN. Goals that are not written down are just something for which you wish, and they lack the commitment that is necessary to make them come true.

To illustrate, Betty and I have a number of goals written down. Some are short-term, some long, but we work towards them together.

- We continue to grow and mature in our relationship with each other;
- Our relationship with all of our children is filled with love, trust, honesty and forgiveness;
- Our financial net worth continues to grow and become more stable;
- Our relationship with our employees is filled with mutual trust and respect;
- We enjoy cruising the Mississippi River and spending time with friends and family (and just ourselves) on our boat;
- Our list of friends with whom we share mutual love and respect continues to grow;

- We have "upgraded" to a van to better accommodate our family needs;
- Our personal relationship with Jesus Christ continues to grow through daily prayer and Bible study;
- I have successfully filled a very important position in our company with someone who is loyal and connected to our business philosophy.

Working toward a common goal can and should be a significant bonding experience. The ultimate reward is when these goals are met, but the steps taken along the way and the plans made can be almost as fulfilling. For Betty and me, working toward and achieving common goals has cemented our relationship. In retrospect, I feel that many times it was the journey toward achieving those goals that actually meant more than accomplishing them. As the saying goes, "getting there is half the fun."

It does not make any difference how old you are or how long or short a time you have been married. Having something to look forward to, both individually and as a couple, only strengthens a relationship.

Let's go back briefly to where I advised writing down your goals. Another advantage to doing so, besides giving you something concrete to study, is that it allows you to pull out those notes every now and then for review. The goals of a newlywed couple are not necessarily the goals or dreams of middle-aged parents. Circumstances and priorities may change. Reviewing these written goals, hopes and dreams allows you to take a look at your life and your relationships. Remember that if you change nothing, nothing changes.

My mother and father, who were 87 and 96 respectively at the time, called me one day out of the blue and told me that they wanted to move to the city we live in. They had spent their entire lives in a small rural community near St. Ansgar, Iowa, yet they had made a decision to move closer to family. Even though there was some anxiety about the change, they assumed the risks because, while living in their hometown and living independent lives once seemed important, now being closer to children and grandchildren meant more. Fortunately for all of us, it turned out to be a very good decision. In your lifetime, decide on something you can look forward to. When that dream becomes a reality, decide on something else.

> What types of goals, hopes, dreams, etc. am I talking about when I encourage you to plan? They can be simple—lose 10 lbs., go blonde, learn French—or they can be more intense—train and complete a marathon, study art in Paris, develop and deliver a stand-up comedy routine for a local club. They can be materialistic—buy a Corvette, get a summer cabin, take a cruise—or more introspective—learn to control my temper, change my work ethic.

While communicating with your children deserves an entire chapter by itself, I do want to discuss how important it is that we, as parents, are on the same track about how we raise our children. I have spent far too many hours counseling parents about their child-rearing practices, and often it is because they had no clear idea of what child-rearing practice they were going to use. The most negative and devastating thing parents can do to a child is to have separate and disagreeing limits and disciplinary methods for that child's behavior. Even if parents are not in complete agreement about their disciplinary styles, they should never let the child see this conflict of values. To do so runs the risk of creating a manipulative personality with whom they, in turn, will experience many negative consequences later in life. In other words, the child will run the family with two fulltime live-in servants.

I recall one particular experience when I observed a child manipulate her parents "to a T." When told by her mother that she was supposed to go to bed, "Suzie" vehemently objected. She proceeded to cuddle up to her father and immediately began to negotiate a deferred bedtime. To my surprise, he gave in and "Suzie" stayed up until she wanted to go to bed.

In my opinion, there are two very strong negatives to what happened. First, you can imagine the potential conflict that the discipline reversal caused between the husband and wife (and rightfully so). Second, "Suzie" has now been positively reinforced that such manipulative behavior works. This type of reinforcement lends itself to developing a scheming and manipulative personality in your child. If you don't think this is serious, let me ask you if you have any adult relationships with someone who is scheming, manipulative, even conniving. Can you honestly say you enjoy being with someone like that?

I strongly encourage would-be as well as active parents to communicate honestly about disciplinary tactics to be used and make every effort to establish agreement. If it seems impossible to totally agree on the limits, restrictions, and disciplinary methods that you place on your children, at least try to find some sort of middle-of-the-road concept acceptable to both of you. Ideally, this should be done before parenthood becomes a reality for you!

Now we get to the good part! I feel that it is extremely important that you communicate with your spouse through the sense of touch. Putting your arm around your spouse, giving a hug, holding a hand, rubbing a neck, etc. speaks volumes. Many people assume that women are particularly gratified by that kind of physical contact, but I think all of us—men and women alike—need the reassurance of touching in our marriages. For those people who seem to have a problem in actually saying the words "I love you," it is even more important to use positive physical contact to communicate that emotion. "I love you," "I like being with you," "I like sharing my life with you" is the non-verbal communication being expressed through touch. Those of you who can both verbalize "I love you" as well as communicate the same feeling through touch, move to the head of the class! I have always felt that a strong characteristic of my marriage has been the unlimited ability to express our love for one another through touch, without any hidden agenda.

There have been hundreds, maybe thousands of books written on the subject of sexual intimacy, or the lack of it, between husband and wife. This will not be another one to put on the shelf. The only thing I would suggest is that communication and closeness play a very important role in this private arena of your lives. Just remember that having or not having sex should never be used as a bargaining tool. Those people who have chosen to use sex as a way of reward or punishment are walking on thin ice. If you want your marriage or relationship to succeed, this ultimate method of expressing affection should be treated like a crystal vase—"Fragile, handle with care!"

CHAPTER SIX

BECAUSE I SAID SO, THAT'S WHY!

Communicating with Your Children

A grandmother and her granddaughter whose face was sprinkled with freckles spent the day at the zoo. The children were waiting in line to get their cheeks painted by an artist when a little boy told the little girl, "You've got so many freckles, there's no place to paint!"

Embarrassed, the little girl dropped her head and her grandmother knelt down beside her.

"I love your freckles," she consoled the child.

"Well, I don't."

"When I was a little girl, I always wanted freckles," her grandmother assured her, tracing her finger across the child's cheek. "Freckles are beautiful."

The little girl looked up.

"Really?"

"Of course. Name me one thing more beautiful than freckles."

The little girl peered into the old woman's smiling face and reached up to pat her cheek.

"Wrinkles," she said.

We can all see things in new and wonderful ways!

Because I Said So, That's Why!

Bringing a child into the world is the most meaningful and significant event anyone can experience. Although these life-changing experiences can bring so much love and joy into your life, they can also be a source of pain and sorrow.

Experiencing the births of our four children were the most meaningful events in my life. Giving birth to a child is also a bonding experience between mother and father. When our first child Tami was born, Betty was in labor for 26 hours and it was quite difficult for her. At the time Tami was born, it was a new practice to allow fathers into the delivery room and I felt so fortunate to experience this miracle. Shortly after Tami's arrival, and in the excitement of the moment, I exclaimed to Betty that this was such a great experience I could hardly wait until we did it again. From the look on Betty's face, I could tell that was the wrong thing to say at the time. As they say, "timing is everything!"

While a new father, I was also in a profession where I worked with troubled children, and I observed first-hand the effects of uninformed and/or unconcerned parenting. I wrote to then President Jimmy Carter, trying to make a strong case for creating some sort of special tax incentive for prospective parents, something to encourage participation in parent training classes prior to a child's birth. It just didn't make any sense to me that we have to take a written and a road test in order to receive a driver's license, or an SAT test to get into college, yet there are no requirements at all to create and bring a new life into the world.

There is no experience in my life that I have loved more than watching my children grow, learning new tasks and, yes, developing their communication skills. Right from the beginning, I was proud to be a father and very proud of my children. For me, being a father to young children was easy and wonderfully delightful. To know you are one of the two most important people in the world to another human being is a coveted role.

I was fortunate to have grown up in a family with strong family ties and values. It was a very happy childhood, and even my adolescence was unmarred by rebellion or anger toward my parents. As I observed my friends working through occasional conflicts with their parents, it made me even more determined to please my parents and make them proud of me.

Our grandparents held certain values that they tried to pass along to our parents; our parents sought to instill those same values in us, and we do what we can to pass them along to our children. It is natural for people who feel confident and positive about the values they have acquired in life to want those same morals and values passed on to their children. For the most part, I feel very good about the positive results of my parenting; however, I know that I fell short at times. Still, Tami, Jody, Leslie and Jason were good children and turned out to be fine adults.

My greatest challenge as a father, like that of many parents, was to accept the unfolding truth that my children would not always have exactly the same values and opinions that I held. There were times when I felt threatened by opposing opinions or characteristics. To accept our children as independent thinkers was something that I was unprepared for. In my own personal, social and business life, I could usually change or improve a situation gone awry because I was in control of my own behavior and feelings. To be unable to control the feelings and behavior of my children was frustrating, yet perhaps (and I would never admit this at the time) somewhat gratifying because I could see them growing into their own identities. As I said earlier, I am very proud of my four adult children and would like to think I had some part in their becoming the fine, upstanding, independent-thinking people they are. They all are successful in their chosen professions, and I love having an adult relationship with each one of them.

What we communicate and how we communicate has the potential for shaping our children's personalities. We can get red hair from Grandma Becky, blue eyes from Dad, musical aptitude from Aunt Sally and height from Grandpa Fred. But our personalities and, more specifically, our communication skills, are the result of learned and observed behavior. And here, as in other aspects of communication, consistency is critical.

For those of you who are reading this book and are parents, ask yourself this: "Does what I communicate to my children reflect the message and actions I communicate to other people? And do those words and actions reflect the values that I consider important?"

If not, you can assume two things:
- Your children will become confused between the message spoken and the non-verbal message observed;
- The message observed comes through louder and more clearly than the message spoken.

Nowhere is this more apparent than in the way parents communicate with each other. The child who grows up in a home where parents effectively resolve differences and where love is generously received and given probably will seek out a life partner with similar characteristics. Similarly, a child raised in a family where anger, discord and violent behavior are common, often ends up assuming that it is the "norm" and will have similar relationships.

Having said all of that, let's now concentrate on some of the most important messages we can communicate to our children.

This may seem like an over-simplification, but I believe we can put the areas that parents need to focus on in terms of communicating with their children into three categories:

1. Love
2. Discipline
3. Values.

Now...how do we do that?

Love

We begin to communicate love to our children from the very first time we pick them up and look into their eyes. During the early stages of life, the most meaningful way we communicate our affection is by touching, hugging and talking to them. As they begin to grow and become more responsive, love is communicated by clapping our hands, smiling, laughing, etc. We communicate love by feeding them, bathing them, and responding to their every want and need. We show love by holding them in our laps and rocking them to sleep, or reading them a book again and again. We have a two-year-old grandson who, after we finish reading him a book, always says "agin." When he says that, I find it very difficult to refuse.

Sometimes I forget that all parents may not love their children the way I love mine. Similarly, I have observed individuals who I thought communicated their love better than I have. What is of utmost importance is that the love you feel towards your children is communicated to them.

Even if you are not religious, there is perhaps no better way to describe the importance of communicating love than from the book written 2000 years ago:

Love is very patient and kind, never jealous or envious, never boastful or proud, never haughty or selfish or rude. Love does not demand its own way......All the special gifts...will someday come to an end, but love goes on forever...there are three things that remain—faith, hope and love—and the greatest of these is love.

I Corinthians, Chapter 13, Verse 4 – 13
The Living Bible, 1971

I think it would be difficult to over-communicate love and affection for your children (unless, of course, you were doing so under false pretenses). Simply stated, it is essential that we use all our senses to communicate this most important of emotions—love—to our children.

We also communicate love through administering proper discipline. I am not talking about "tough love" situations. I am talking about discipline that guides our children through infancy and their formative years by giving them behavioral boundaries and consequences for exceeding those boundaries. This discipline delivers a message to them over the years that says "I love you." After all, if we didn't love our children, we wouldn't care how they turned out.

Discipline

Communicating discipline is much more complicated and, certainly, the area in which I have observed more problems, misunderstandings and conflict. Because of my profession, many times I observed the negative consequences that resulted from either an abuse of discipline, or a lack of discipline entirely.

Whether you are a couple or a single parent, it is very important that you devote a considerable amount of time in deciding how and what kind of disciplinary methods you will use with your children. Communicate clearly and often to each other about this so that you are "on the same page" and will support each other in disciplinary strategies.

Once that decision is made, it is of utmost importance that you be consistent. As a counselor, I told people that it was more important that they be consistent in applying questionable disciplinary methods than if they were inconsistent in using great methods. The message you communicate by being inconsistent leads to confusion that, in turn, lends itself to manipulative behavior. You do not want to create a manipulative personality in your children. It will cause hardship for you and them, both when they are young and when they are older.

If you cannot agree on behavioral boundaries and what disciplinary actions will take place, make every effort not to show that in front of your children. The child who observes his or her parents disagreeing about discipline learns quickly how to manipulate those adults into getting his or her own way.

Example: Mary is allowed one soda pop a day, usually during a meal. One evening after dinner and before bedtime, Mary asks for a second cola. Her mother says no, she chose to have her drink at lunchtime. Unhappy with the decision, Mary decides to go to her father to see if she can negotiate another soda from him. She crawls up in Daddy's lap, gives him a big hug, and he gives in to her request and gets her another drink from the kitchen. Mary has successfully negotiated a new arrangement with her father and negated Mother's ruling.

What was communicated in this instance?
- Mary now knows that she can successfully pit one parent against the other;
- Mary realizes that her parents are not consistent on this issue and that this same inconsistency will most likely be prevalent in other issues;
- Father has communicated, both to Mary and her mother, that he is not willing to support his wife on behavioral

boundaries. This kind of inconsistency undercuts her disciplinary efforts and can easily cause conflict between the parents.

- Father has communicated to Mary that with some sweet talk and loving behavior, he can be influenced to change his mind.

Mary has them both right where she wants them—letting *her* set the rules.

What would be a better response in this situation, one that would communicate consistency in discipline? Father should say to Mary, "Honey, you know the rules about only one soda each day. Today you decided to have your drink with lunch. Tomorrow you can plan ahead and choose to have your soda at either lunch or dinner. You'll have to pick." Such a response indicates to Mary that pitting one parent against the other will not work, that sweet talk will not result in deviation from the accepted discipline, and that both parents are looking out for Mary's well being.

Example: Mother takes Amy, age 4, and Justin, age 2, into the grocery store and almost immediately they begin to fight with each other. Mother tells Amy and Justin that if they don't stop fighting with each other and crying, she will take them to the car. They continue to fight. Mother tells them once again that if they continue to fight, she will take them to the car. By now, they are really making a lot of noise. This continues for 20 minutes while Mother continues to shop and issue dire warnings.

The communicated message?

- Mother does not mean what she says, and the children wonder where else this might apply;

- Mother is not in control;
- Discipline won't be enforced in public places and the children can dictate the rules.

In situations like this, it is so important that parents never communicate any proposed disciplinary measure if they are not prepared to follow through with it. In this case, after Mother had issued her initial warning—behave or we're leaving—if the two children again began to fight, Mother should have parked her grocery cart and left the store with both children. It would have been an inconvenience to a mother who was probably already running short on time and would now have to plan another time to shop, and it might have even been an embarrassment if Amy and Justin began to throw a "hissy-fit." But it would communicate to the children that Mother meant what she said, that such behavior was unacceptable in a public place, and it would happen again and again until they learned to listen and respect her. In the long run, although such an exercise might have to be repeated few times before it sinks in, the children will learn that there are boundaries and there are consequences for exceeding those boundaries. Believe me, everyone will be happier.

"Say What You Do and Do What You Say!"

These nine simple words should be at the core of every form of communication you have with your children. We tried very hard to be true to ourselves in demonstrating this most serious form of communication to our children. If you were to ask our adult children today if we were consistent in what we told them we would do if certain behavior was exhibited and in what we actually ended up doing, I think they would tell you that we were. That's not to say they agreed with everything we said or did!

Raising responsible and well-behaved kids is not a popularity contest. Sometimes the most important communication of love to your children is to be willing to enforce unpopular decisions. We communicate love through affection, but we can also communicate love through properly administered discipline. Appropriate discipline is what establishes boundaries for our behavior, and through discipline we receive feedback on what behavior is acceptable and what is not.

While the arduous task of raising children is not an exact science, I do believe there are some very effective methods that can be used, and I believe there are some very ineffective and counterproductive methods that are being used.

First of all, Betty and I were on the same page in regards to what we expected in terms of appropriate behavior. In addition, we agreed on what we felt to be appropriate discipline. We tried very hard to administer disciplinary measures without exhibiting anger and hostility, and while I must confess that we were not always successful in leaving our emotions out of our corrective measures, we tried as best we could to utilize the concept of logical consequences—"If you do 'A', then 'B' will happen to you." This concept is successful because there is a direct correlation between the inappropriate behavior and the disciplinary measure. More importantly, it totally eliminates the inclusion of any strong emotions from the parents. Let me give you a couple of examples.

Once while in the park with our family, our oldest daughter Tami was throwing small rocks at her younger sister. They were, as I recall, about 8 and 6 respectively. We told her to stop doing it and if she did not heed our warning she would be punished. To our surprise, she continued to pursue this unconventional form of entertainment, so I said, "Tami, it appears that you really enjoy throwing things, so we are going to have you throw this empty pop can against the side of the building for thirty minutes." In this case, we connected the discipline—throwing something—to the misbehavior of throwing rocks at her sister. The beauty of this exchange was that we were able to implement a disciplinary method without expressing any emotion. The discipline was effective and I do not recall Tami ever throwing anything at her siblings again (at least not where we could see her!).

Another example occurred when, once again, our oldest daughter decided to give her younger sister a haircut. Upon our discovery of this unsightly procedure, we told Tami that it was obvious she liked to use a scissors for cutting things, so it was now her responsibility to cut up the newspaper into 1" x 3" strips. It took her the better part of an hour to accomplish that task. By the time she had completed the logical consequence of her behavior, her desire for using a scissors inappropriately had sufficiently disappeared.

You may have noticed that in both of these examples, our oldest daughter was the recipient of our disciplinary action. If you happen to be the oldest child in your family, you most likely outscored your younger siblings in the number of times your parents made attempts at altering your behavior. It is true in most families of multiple children that the oldest child breaks the way for what is to be determined as acceptable or unacceptable behavior. In our situation, I think our younger three children observed and absorbed our reactions to what we deemed unacceptable behavior and knew we meant it! Sorry about that, Tami.

As I mentioned earlier, whether you use logical consequence or behavior modification, make every attempt to eliminate emotion from your discipline. By doing so, you communicate to your children that you disapprove of certain behavior, but continue to love the child.

Values

"Values" is an all-inclusive word that can and does mean a lot of things. There are so many areas and aspects of our lives in which we develop an attitude or place a value. A value is something we feel has worth to others and us. It can be tangible, such as family and friends, or it can be unseen such as a system of ethics, morals or even attitudes. Most of our values originate from what our parents or other significant people communicate to us during the formative years when we are growing up.

Some of what I consider to be core values for living a fulfilling and successful life are: love and affection, interests, activities, and attitudes toward money.

Love and Affection

Whether you realize it or not, you have developed and placed a value on how you feel about love and affection. Your parents communicated to you the value they have placed on this emotion by the way in which they showed love and affection to you and the way in which they expressed love and affection for each other, their families, friends and co-workers.

You observed and absorbed those feelings. What your parents communicated to you regarding love and affection had a great deal to do with how you show love and affection to the people in your life today. And, of course, how you communicate love and affection to your children and those around you contributes immensely to the value your children place on those emotions.

I think it is important to begin saying the words "I love you" early and often. Of course, just saying the words is not enough. It is the feeling, the look in your eyes, the tone of your voice and the touch of your hands, along with the words, that give true meaning and value to those three words. As children get older, we do not say the words as often as we do earlier in life; however, I hope we continue to communicate it in other ways.

Interests, Activities and Hobbies
More than likely, a lot of the interests, activities and hobbies we possess came by observing our parents and others. Just for fun, make a mental list of the main activities and hobbies that are a part of your life today. How many of them are similar to those of your parents? If you did not gain interest in those activities and hobbies from your parents, can you recall where they came from? Perhaps you collect antique glass because your mother did. Maybe you spend time on the river because your parents took you there every Sunday afternoon. Or maybe you are building a model train set because a favorite uncle had

one in the basement. Somewhere along the line, someone communicated to you an enthusiasm for the interests, hobbies and activities that are important to you today.

As parents, we also play a very important role in communicating to our children the attitude and the intensity with which we approach and participate in these special interests in our lives.

Money

Nothing elicits a wider range of reactions than people's attitudes about money. We love it, we hate it, we rely on it, we curse being tied to it, we use it, we hoard it. What is your value toward having and spending money? Where did it come from? Can you trace back into your past and determine where you developed the value you place on money? I strongly suspect that your parents indicated to you in a variety of ways the value they placed on money. How frugal or liberal they were with their money and how effective or ineffective they were in saving and investing certainly had an effect on you.

In counseling adults, I discovered that money was often the direct or indirect cause of conflict. Therefore, I think it is critical that you clearly communicate to your children the core values you hold about money.

In raising our children, we felt it was important to give them a weekly allowance. We wanted to let them know that their allowance was a form of showing appreciation for responsibly fulfilling their daily chores. Giving them an allowance at an early age transferred responsibility to them for making decisions on what and how they were going to spend the money. It encouraged them to save, if necessary, to purchase a more expensive item. Even though I am sure our children did not feel their allowance was large enough, through this strategy we were able to demonstrate the necessity of developing responsible spending habits. It communicated the value of making wise and prudent choices between those things they wanted and those things they could actually afford. Finally, it eliminated the need for us as parents to make choices between what they wanted and what they purchased. We didn't have to take on the role of "Scrooge" because the responsibility fell primarily to them.

There were times when we would put a dollar value on the completion of some special task that needed to be done around the house. Here we were trying to communicate that there was both a verbal and monetary reward for fulfilling a task, a direct correlation between effort and reward.

Betty and I have planned and worked very hard for the rewards and possessions that we now have. The things we now are able to do and have takes on a greater meaning and value to us because we know in our hearts that we have earned and deserve them. We want to communicate to our children (and hope that they will pass it on) the value of obtaining a positive reward for diligence and effort. When I see parents giving their children almost everything they want, it concerns me because doing so does not teach them anything (except perhaps how to whine or pout if they don't get an item). It concerns me even more when I see parents giving their adult children all kinds of possessions they could not afford on their own. I believe it is the wrong value to communicate and, more importantly, it deprives those young adults of the wonderful gratification of actually earning something by their own hard work.

Way to Grow!

How and what we communicate to our children changes as they grow and develop. During each stage of a child's development, it is important that parents respond to those developmental changes and alter the level of communication accordingly. As parents, we help shape our children's personalities by what we communicate to them as they grow in their ability to understand feelings and emotions. It is essential that we recognize what words, feelings and emotions represent to a child, and that we change how we communicate as their level of maturity changes. For example, asking your son "Do you like the girl who sits next to you at school?" will elicit a different response when he is five than it will when he is a teen-ager.

During the early stages of development, our children are too busy learning about their world to question the words or ideas of a parent. However, as they grow and mature in their own relationships, they no longer accept our thoughts and words blindly. How we adapt to their ongoing development and how we adjust the way we communicate with them will determine how successful we are in maintaining positive and meaningful relationships.

Adolescence and mood swings just seem to go together. In both my counseling practice and in my own experience as a father, I discovered that! The degree and length of moods varies from child to child. I often felt as if I were in the middle of a tropical storm season. One minute it would be bright and sunny, then rain clouds would appear out of nowhere. I'd "batten down the hatches" and prepare logically for the onslaught, only to have the tempest suddenly change course and veer out to sea. I'd shake my head, breathe a sigh of relief, and turn around—only to get hit in the face with an unexpected squall from a different direction! It was disconcerting, to say the least.

There were times when I found it difficult to find the right words to say to ease the conflict. Sometimes even silence was wrong!

Looking back at those years, I realize that it would have been better had I expressed less disapproval of minor departures from my expectations. I do believe that children, particularly as they emerge into and work their way through adolescence, need to be allowed a healthy degree of latitude, as long as they stay within the moral and value boundaries you have established. "Don't sweat the small stuff," as they say.

It is particularly important during the adolescent years to keep the lines of communication open, which also includes being able to say you are sorry and, perhaps even more important, to be able to forgive and forget.

As a parent, one of the things you hope and pray for is that your children can emerge from adolescence into adulthood without making any negative life-changing decisions. In today's world, adolescents face many challenges—drugs, alcohol, teen pregnancy, school violence, etc. As parents, it is up to us to see that our children make safe and informed choices when faced with these potentially life-changing decisions. What and how we communicate to our children during their adolescent years is very important. If you have adolescent children today and you are experiencing communication problems, I encourage you to seek help from professionals who can guide you through these challenging experiences. Once again, Grandma's advice is the best—an ounce of prevention is worth a pound of cure.

For those of you with children who have incurred a negative life-changing experience during adolescence, I do have some words of encouragement. I personally know several families where children's decisions during those years derailed them from their original and desired life's journey. In many of these situations, because the parents kept communicating love and support, the children are now living positive, fulfilling lives. Parents and children are once again enjoying positive relationships. What and how parents communicated during those trying times enabled the family to remain supportive. Always remember, our words during challenging times can be poison or fertilizer for our relationships with our children. Choose them carefully.

Before I close this chapter, I would like to share some examples of the more positive communication experiences that we had with our children.

Betty and I always found that planned vacation time with our family provided some of the best and most positive experiences in communication. It is very important to set aside time for a family vacation on an annual basis. Vacation means a period of time when you "vacate" from daily routine and responsibilities, and this alone sets the stage for positive and meaningful conversations.

Each year we would plan a winter and a summer vacation. If they coincided with school vacations that was fine, but Betty and I and our children's teachers never thought taking our children out of school for a week was a negative use of their time. Our children gained more knowledge during those weeks than they ever could have in a classroom setting. Please don't interpret this as being a criticism of our education system. It is, rather, an indication of how important I feel it is to have special, meaningful experiences with your children outside the boundaries of normal, daily routines. How rewarding to learn about our country and our world by actually seeing it first-hand and being a part of it!

The places, events and experiences of our traveling ventures were great. They represented positive learning experiences and education-enhancing opportunities that are difficult to duplicate in the classroom. However, the conversations we shared around campfires, in the car while traveling, or during a picnic lunch are what I remember to be the most meaningful. It was during those times that the children (and the entire family) seemed more inclined to share their feelings and emotions, and they felt comfortable to ask our opinions on a variety of subjects. To those still in the child-rearing stage of life, I strongly encourage you to set aside time and money to create some positive, memorable experiences for you and your children.

In an earlier chapter, I pointed out the importance of occasionally scheduling some time away for just you and your spouse. I repeat that advice here even more emphatically. Remember, the most important gift you can give your children is a healthy marriage. It was during those times of peace and quiet and relaxation that Betty and I had some of our most meaningful and memorable conversations.

We had other family routines that we diligently tried to maintain. It was a rule in our house to eat breakfast together. We chose breakfast because it seemed the least difficult of all meals to share together. Time permitting, we would have a short devotion before everyone left. I realize that with work schedules, school, etc. this can be a difficult agenda to adhere to, but it is one more opportunity to communicate as a family and you can never have too many of those!

We also made an effort to have one specially-prepared family evening meal together each week. At the end of this meal, we would hold a short "family meeting" to discuss the events that took place during the previous week between siblings and/or parent and child. Sitting together as a family, we would discuss any problems or challenges that were being faced and how to deal with them best. It was also during this time that we would evaluate how everyone had done in completing weekly job assignments. Each week we changed who was in charge of the meeting in an attempt to give each one of our children the opportunity to lead a discussion. It was our hope that some of these leadership skills developed at home could be transferred to other groups outside of the home. Don't get me wrong—we weren't setting out to have our four children walking around carrying a copy of Roberts Rules of Order. We simply wanted them to feel comfortable and confident in a leadership role.

I have shared these examples with you to let you know how important it is to create opportunities for meaningful communication. Not everyone needs to duplicate the same events or experiences we shared, but as parents you need to make a special effort to create opportunities and experiences that lend themselves to meaningful, positive communication within your own family environment.

If formal vacations aren't always possible, there are still unlimited opportunities for parents to "get away" with their children and communicate. You could:

- Go to a county or city park for a picnic, then spend time playing games like follow-the-leader, hide n' seek, etc.;
- Go fishing at a local river or lake, followed by a fish fry (or hot dog roast if the fishing wasn't that great) on the beach;
- Visit a children's museum in your area;
- If you live in a city, drive out to the country for the day and tour a farm. If you're a rural family, check out a nearby "big city" and explore;
- Attend a movie together, followed by pizza and roller-skating;
- Check out several books on stars at your library, then see how many constellations and planets you can see after dark;
- Go biking as a family, bringing along a picnic lunch. There are many places that rent all types of bicycles these days so that everyone can go along;
- Locate a hiking trail and make a day of studying nature;
- Cheer on your favorite team at a sporting event while you all dress in team colors.

The list of things to do is limited only by your imagination. If you're the adventuresome type, have each family member make two or three suggestions for family outings, write them on slips of paper and then draw one a week, month, etc. The key is planning far enough in advance so that no one has any excuse for not participating and everyone can look forward to spending time together.

To borrow an analogy from my rural roots, you can't just drop seeds on the ground and expect them to grow properly. You must first prepare the soil, cultivating and fertilizing it in order for the seeds to have a good spot to be nourished. Good communication with your children doesn't just happen, either. You need to do all you can to create favorable environments for that communication to take place and for strong, positive relationships with your children to grow and flourish.

CHAPTER SEVEN

WORKING NINE TO FIVE

Communicating on the Job

One day a middle management fellow was promoted to vice president. Early Monday morning, he strode down the hall towards his new office. Finding a younger man waiting outside his door, the man puffed up and told him to wait while he made an important phone call.

He walked into his office, closed the door and loudly pretended to be speaking on the phone.

"Yes sir, Senator, I'll pass along your message to the Board of Directors this afternoon."

He then stepped outside the office and turned to the waiting man.

"And what can I do for you?"

The young man smiled faintly.

"I'm here to connect your phone."

Honesty is always the best policy!

Communicating On The Job

Whether you are an employee, employer, business partner or business associate, and whether you deal with the public or behind the scenes, communicating effectively on the job is vital to your success.

Our jobs, where we work, who we employ, who our business associates are, and the degree of personal and financial success we achieve on the job play a very important role in how positively or negatively we view our lives. Often, the attitude we have about our work environment says a lot about the attitude we have in life. One of the saddest things I have witnessed on the job is the person who, first thing on a Monday morning, is looking forward to the weekend! To me, that implies that they are simply "killing time" on the job and they feel no sense of fulfillment or challenge in what is, for most people, a very large part of their lives.

While growing up on the farm, I learned the value and meaning of hard work. I believe in working hard, and I have a strong work ethic. I also have a firm belief in enjoying myself, that there is "a time to work and a time to play," and you should enjoy both

In a sense, I have been "researching" this chapter for many years. Along my various career paths, I have accumulated a variety of experiences, good and bad, which have all served as learning opportunities for me. Like other successful people, I have been very fortunate in reaping the positive rewards of hard work, commitment and dedication. As most successful people will tell you, becoming successful does not just happen and is certainly not the result of being lucky. Most successful businesspeople have certain traits in common—the ability and willingness to work hard, the ability to focus on specific goals and ways to achieve them, and—here it comes—the ability to communicate effectively.

Many of the communication skills I learned and developed in my social work training and professional experience benefited me in a positive way while on the job. Developing some sense of knowing when, what, and how to communicate certain ideas or thoughts plays an important role in being successful at any level of employment. And listening, which is critical to successful communication, is important in any meaningful relationship and certainly an important skill to employ in the workplace.

While there are several similarities in the use and value of good communication skills, whether you are an employee, employer or business partner, there are also some unique differences. Let's look at the similarities first.

If you are successful in communications in your personal, social and family relationships, you have a good chance of being successful in developing strong positive relationships while at work. Similarly, if you are unable to adequately communicate on a personal, social and family basis, there is a good chance that you will have difficulties on the job. In general, making every attempt to be respectful, honest, loyal, dedicated and sensitive to the feelings and emotions of others, demonstrating all the while a strong work ethic, will pay positive dividends for you.

Most of the complaints I hear from people who are unhappy in their work environment stem from something someone said or did not say—in other words, communication! Think of a time when your workplace or work environment became unpleasant or uncomfortable and, therefore, unproductive. Chances are, you can trace that negativity to something someone said or did not say. Were instructions vague? Were deadlines and timeframes misstated? Were individual job responsibilities unclear or unassigned? Was hard work and individual or team efforts unacknowledged? It has been my experience that the better the communication is in the workplace, the happier the employees are and the smoother the job goes.

Employee

Following graduation from graduate school, I was an employee in three different settings over fifteen years. I enjoyed my role and position in each one of these environments, developing meaningful relationships with my colleagues and a mutually respectful relationship with my superiors. In these instances, effort and hard work were required on my part.

With my superiors or boss, I made a conscious effort to communicate my respect for their role, and I was particularly careful to communicate my subservience to their positions. This does not mean I never questioned or challenged any of their thoughts or decisions, but if I felt a need to do so, I would communicate my thoughts and/or objections in a non-threatening and non-hostile way. Wherever possible, I would try to find something about which I could sincerely offer a compliment to them—"building them up," so to speak. Most importantly, when given an assignment, I would make sure that

I would meet or exceed their expectations of me, completing the work on time and as required. Failing to follow through on an assigned task is a very negative form of communication.

If you were to ask a variety of employers what quality they value most in an employee, the majority of them would probably indicate "reliability." A key part of reliability is being on time. This is a critical part of non-verbal communication on the job. Being on time for a meeting or a sales call should be a top priority. Someone who is late, particularly those who have a chronic habit of not showing up on time, demonstrates to those who are waiting a lack of professionalism and of consideration for the other person's time. Failure to be prompt can very often be a prerequisite for deteriorating employee/employer and/or peer relationships.

As with any relationship, it is vital to communicate some degree of interest into the personal life of your superiors. We aren't talking about discussing the private details of a supervisor's life or doing an interview for CNN. Instead, think of all the "common ground" you might share with a boss or superior. "Did you have a good weekend, Mr. Smith?" "That was quite a game Sunday. Are you a Packer fan, Mr. Jones?" "Were you able to get out and play golf this weekend, Mrs. Adams?" After you have received a few responses to this kind of casual communication, you may be able to ask more specific questions about personal and family life.

A word of caution here, along with a gentle reminder: Always remember that you are in a workplace and not a coffee shop. Casual small talk about family and personal matters is fine, but this is not the time nor the place to go into in-depth discussions about your health, co-workers, the boss, etc. First, it is inappropriate. Second, you never know who may be listening and be offended or hurt by your conversation. And third, it is a sad fact of life that some people may use information you shared in confidence to further their own position within a company. If you feel comfortable enough with a co-worker to share the intimate details of your life (or theirs), then meet socially outside the workplace and do so. If someone tries to hold such a conversation with you, simply say, "Amy, I'm really too busy to talk about this now. Let's meet after work and grab a bite."

Look for things about which you can compliment your superiors. As long as your compliments are deemed sincere and not an attempt to "brown nose" someone, they will be accepted and appreciated. And remember not to overdo the compliments or they will lose their value and meaning.

There's a popular song from the 50's (ahhh, they don't write music like that anymore!) that encourages us to "accentuate the positive" and "eliminate the negative," and nowhere is that more applicable than in the workplace. No one enjoys being around someone who is complaining about something all the time. If you are guilty of ongoing negative comments or "pessimistic syndrome," I encourage you to think long and hard about changing your attitude. It is just a fact of life that we have to take the bad with the good. I seriously doubt that anyone can say there is nothing they dislike about their job. Don't ignore negative experiences, but try to focus on and emphasize the positive experiences of your job. How much time you spend on communicating the negative aspects of your job will set the tone for your conversations—you just have to determine that positive is better.

Whatever you do, if you are discontent or dissatisfied with your job, please try to avoid involving other people in your dissatisfaction. Unless your negative attitude is a common denominator (i.e., most of your co-workers are equally as unhappy with some situation), trying to persuade someone to share your negativity is doing a disservice to them, the company, and yourself.

If your negative feelings seem overwhelming, then do something! As an employer, I was always ready to listen to a worker's complaints, but I was truly interested when someone presented me with solutions or suggestions for improvement along with the complaint. Let's say you work in a manufacturing facility that operates 8:00 AM to 4:00 PM and you're never able to get home in time to attend your son's tee ball games. Instead of grumbling about company policy and letting your resentment and negative feelings build, put together a plan to present to management that outlines and explains why flexible work hours might be an option. Or perhaps you could work through the lunch hour, covering phones and others' absences in exchange for being allowed to leave at 3:30. Being able to clearly and effectively communicate what the problem is, and being able to offer sensible, well thought out solutions, is a skill any employer would welcome. Remember, though, you are an employee and the company is not there to make your life easier but to allow you to make a living.

You know from other relationships that it is important to establish meaningful ways of resolving conflicts. The worst thing you can do is to allow disagreements and hurt feelings to fester and grow. Sometimes the most difficult part of resolving a conflict is knowing how to approach the subject.

First of all, closely examine the basis of your negative feelings. Are they legitimate, or were you simply having a bad day when the "offense" took place? Should you feel as upset with that person or people as you do? Often, sharing the incident that upset you with someone else helps you determine if your feelings are justified. On many occasions, I would give Betty a detailed description of something that had upset me and why I was upset (okay, I was really dumping on her!), and she would be able to dilute or deflect my negative feelings, showing me where I might have misread or misinterpreted something.

After you have examined and considered your negative feelings thoughtfully, you may decide that the incident or situation still needs to be addressed. Begin by evaluating different methods of handling the matter. If it involves a co-worker or peer, can it be handled between the two of you or will it be necessary to include a supervisor? Is a formal meeting necessary or would casual discussion be better? Remember that the compelling reason for dealing with any negative situation is to sustain a positive and meaningful relationship with the people involved.

How you approach the subject will have a lot to do with the outcome. When the timing and setting seem appropriate, you might say something like, "Remember the other day when you said…I'm not sure what you meant by this, but the way I took it made me feel…" Or, "I would like to talk to you about what happened the other day. I just don't have a good feeling about what happened." Or, "Sam, could we talk about what happened between us Friday? I think we need to clear the air." It has been my experience that the most difficult part of this process is approaching the subject, but once I've done so, it was not that difficult to talk about it. Remember that if you feel or sense there are negative vibrations between you and someone else, you can almost bet that the other person is feeling it too and will welcome the chance to resolve the matter.

Resolving conflicts is where good communication can shine. Too many people harbor negative feelings that can and do give life to an infectious disease that often results in a terminal relationship. I encourage you not to let that happen to you, whether it be in a personal or a business relationship.

Being a good team player is what every employer looks for in a good employee. How well you communicate your desire to be part of the team will positively contribute to the work environment. To communicate divisiveness gives breath to a negative work culture, affects productivity, and certainly affects the way you feel when you go home. If you feel negative about the place you work and the job you do, try to resolve your differences and make some positive decisions about how you contribute to making your workplace a more pleasant and positive place. If you are simply unable to do so, perhaps you should start looking for another job.

Employer

Looking back, I think I truly began to recognize the value of good communication skills when I became an employer. Many experiences and lessons learned about communication motivated me to write an entire book on the subject. For me, myself, and I, good communication was a necessary prerequisite for being a business owner. I feel that my communication skills have been challenged and tested more in this area of my life than in any other. There have been negative experiences and some disappointments, certainly, and I'm sure there have been any number of people disappointed in me, but for the most part, my experiences in this role have been positive and enriching.

Over the past twenty years, I have employed many different people with a wide range of educational levels, backgrounds and skills. Communicating with manual laborers might vary in some ways from communicating with college-educated people, but the basic attitudes and values do not.

For me, whether or not you can get other people—your employees—to buy into what you believe and what is important to you is the most important goal any employer should have if he/she wants to be successful in business.

As an employer, your success depends, in part, on how clearly you can communicate your goals and your "vision" of how you see the company operating. This can best be described and translated into the "values" you hold and how well you can communicate those values to others. Let me re-emphasize a point that you should never forget, no matter where you are in the corporate or workplace structure. What you communicate is not always expressed in words. Actions, as they say, speak louder than words, and you must demonstrate your commitment and vision through your actions.

What are some necessary values that you need to communicate—in words and actions—as you work for success?

1. *HONESTY* - It is critical that an employer who wants to recruit and retain good employees be someone in whom those employees can trust and believe. No one wants to be a part of something if he/she cannot be sure that an employer is telling the truth.

    There may be times as an employer when it is difficult to communicate "the whole truth and nothing but the truth." This usually involves bad news (maybe lay-offs, reduced earnings, etc.) or information of a sensitive nature (perhaps potential sales, mergers, etc.) In those cases, it is important that you consciously think through how, what, and when is the best way to impart news, bearing in mind that it should be in a truthful manner. The one thing an employer should never do is to lie about a situation. More than likely, dishonest communication will come back to haunt you in the form of gossip, rumors, and bad feelings. It is just not worth it, regardless of how difficult it may be to be truthful at all times. The employer who is discovered lying once—no matter how seemingly insignificant the matter—will have a hard time regaining the trust of employees. Remember, it is better to keep quiet about a matter than to lie about it.

    Part of your responsibility as an employer is to make decisions regarding what information can be shared and when. As an employer, I know there are any number of times when circumstances dictated that I not tell an employee everything about a situation. If I felt that sharing certain information would be counterproductive, I would simply tell the employee, "Right now I would prefer not to discuss the details of that situation with you. If and when the time comes that you should be privy to that information, I'll let you know." That approach is much more desirable than being dishonest with them, and I like to think that my decisions have been respected by my employees.

2. *COMMITMENT* - As an employer, I believe it is essential that you both verbally and non-verbally demonstrate a strong commitment to the *mission* of your company. Are you committed to providing the best service and/or product to your customers that you possibly can? More importantly, how do you communicate that level of commitment to your employees? Your words and actions must reflect that commitment or else, sooner or later, your employees' performance will reflect that unconcern. As clichéd as it sounds, you are the captain of the ship and everyone is looking to you for guidance on how to make the voyage a success. Commitment means hard work, and as an employer, you set the tone by the degree of effort you exhibit.

A mission statement is a brief and concise summary of the purpose of your company. It is a roadmap of where a corporation or business is headed and how it intends to get there. Mission statements can be as varied as the companies they represent, but, just to give you an idea, here is the Mission Statement for Kitchen Solvers.

> *Kitchen Solvers is committed to providing small business entrepreneurs the opportunity to improve the quality of their life by fulfilling the dream of owning a business. Kitchen Solvers is dedicated to providing a proven system with a commitment to excellence through training and on-going support services to each individual franchise.*
>
> The value of a mission statement is that it gives you a clearly understood goal or goals, something to focus on as day-to-day corporate policies and practices are constructed.

3. *VISION* - The vision you have for your company provides a road map for where your company will go, but communicating that vision to your employees is only the beginning. Vision by itself has no meaning unless you can successfully communicate that you believe in and are committed to seeing it become a reality.

   Several years ago, when Betty and I still owned the Kitchen Solvers' franchise in La Crosse, Wisconsin, I challenged our staff to a lofty sales volume goal for the month of March. In addition to the other ongoing responsibilities I had, I felt it was important that I communicate my commitment to that goal. So I took several appointments myself and made a number of sales. As a team, we reached and exceeded what had seemed an impossible goal. I think my commitment to the goal elevated everyone else's level of commitment and, as a result, we were able to experience the positive results and rewards of working hard to achieve a common goal.

As CEO of Kitchen Solvers, I feel very fortunate to know that my associates buy into my vision as much as they do. When we are successful, when we have a record-breaking month or add a new franchise, everyone experiences a healthy degree of pride and seems to recommit to the vision. I believe that they believe in Kitchen Solvers' mission statement –and me—because I believe in them!

Just as a little personal note: After a few negative experiences with employees, I implemented a plan of hiring people that I already knew, friends and/or business associates. I knew that their values and morals were similar to mine and, more importantly, I knew how they communicated with other people. Communication in our business is extremely important as we build and grow relationships with our customers and franchisees. Therefore, I knew I had to employ associates who could communicate well and believed in Betty and me. This practice has resulted in 0% turnover in 12 years! My philosophy is that it is less difficult to teach a trade or a skill to someone than it is to teach them how to communicate effectively.

As is the practice with many companies, the people who work for Kitchen Solvers are called "associates" rather than "employees." The term "associates" represents fewer rungs on the business ladder and communicates commitment to each other and the company in a better way.

4. *PRAISE* - There are any number of surveys and studies to indicate that receiving praise or the occasional pat on the back means more to an employee than a salary increase. During troubled economic times that may not hold quite as true, but I know how important it is to freely communicate praise and acknowledge hard work on the part of employees. Tell your employees that you are pleased with their efforts, and that it means something to the company. "Bob, that was a well-written proposal you submitted." "Sam, I really appreciate the way you got that last-minute order filled." "Karen, I don't think our office would run as smoothly if you weren't managing it." If you look closely at your company and its employees, you shouldn't have to look far to find reasons to sincerely compliment people. If you do, then maybe you should look at whether or not you have the right people in the right jobs. And remember, there is only one thing worse than never giving your employees praise and that is giving empty, insincere praise. Folks, that is a no-no!!

It is extremely valuable to compliment and praise others in the presence of their peers or family members. Once Betty and I were at a restaurant and I had an opportunity to compliment one of our associates in front of several of his family members. The next day he made a point of telling me how much those words of praise had meant to him. Complimenting employees in front of their peers often strengthens the feeling of teamwork among them, and motivates others to do the same. If done appropriately, hearing others being praised for their efforts can serve as an incentive to be more committed and to work harder.

Often compliments are given spontaneously, yet there are other times when it is important to think about how and what would be the most effective praise to offer. Compliments mean different things to different people. Think through how you perceive each person in terms of what is important to him /her. The reason you are praising that individual and the words you use should be unique to that person and his/her circumstances.

For example, after you get to know an associate or employee well, it should become apparent to you what kind of compliment or words of praise mean the most to that individual. For some people, it may mean making positive comments about the clothes they wear or a new hairstyle. For others, it may mean complimenting them on the way they handled a difficult customer on the phone or on how many hours they worked to complete a task. Your praise should be as varied as the people for whom it is meant.

5. *FUN* - What you communicate to your employees about having fun and being relaxed in the workplace carries a lot of weight and has far-reaching effects. Our annual Kitchen Solvers' Christmas party is a wonderful time not only to share words of praise and hand out compliments, but also to take a look at some of the funny things that happened during

the year. Often, we present small gifts—gag gifts—that remind people of something funny that happened. The general reaction and comments indicate how important it is to everyone in our office that we maintain a fun atmosphere.

We're not talking about balloons and confetti at everyone's desk, and having a "fun" atmosphere does not imply an absence of hard work and commitment. What it does mean is that we have created an environment where people feel comfortable and relaxed. We can tease each other, tell appropriate jokes and, above all else, be willing to laugh at ourselves. We tend not to "sweat the small stuff" and concentrate instead on providing quality sales and service to our customers. Think about it—have you ever called a business or an office and "heard" someone smiling when the phone was answered? Didn't that make you feel good? That person reflected a relaxed atmosphere, a place where people felt good about themselves and (hopefully) about their jobs.

In sharp contrast, one of my personal pet peeves is places—primarily check-out counters—where a neatly-typed sign is taped to the cash register admonishing the clerk to "Smile–smile–smile." Being told to smile and actually wanting to smile are two vastly different things and will be reflected in job performance and productivity.

Sharing a joke or appropriate teasing of each other can build a spirit of camaraderie between individuals who work in the same office or workplace. By "appropriate teasing," I mean the kind of teasing that avoids making everyone else laugh at the expense of another person. If you sense that your attempts at humor either offend or hurt others, then forget it. Similarly, if you observe another employee doing the same, it is best to put a stop to it at once.

Having fun at work can give you more energy as you focus on individual responsibilities. Creating a fun atmosphere does not have to fall on the shoulders of the owner, but allowing and encouraging workers to share laughter during work hours is something you can—and should—do. Employees who feel comfortable enough to have fun usually feel comfortable enough to exchange ideas, venture opinions and, thus, work for the common good of the company.

6. *CONSTRUCTIVE CRITICISM* - Although I am seldom faced with this problem anymore, I have read a lot on how to deal with those situations where an associate or an employee is not adequately fulfilling his/her job responsibilities. (Ken Blanchard's *The One Minute Manager* is an excellent source.) It is quite evident that the successful employer is one who develops—and implements—a well thought-out strategy for dealing with unacceptable performance and makes certain that policy is communicated clearly to all employees.

When dealing with lower-than-expected performance, the approach that I have found to be most effective is to deal with it quickly, directly and specifically, then leave it. Judge that employee's performance from that day forward without letting past behavior or results influence your evaluations. Everyone deserves the chance to correct negative behaviors. As an employer, you must provide opportunities to do so, first by pointing out where the problem lies, and secondly, by giving employees the tools and direction to change.

For example, if Alfred turns in a monthly sales report that is inadequate, you can call him in, criticize the poorly-done report and turn him loose in the office again. Or you can meet with Alfred privately, explain in detail what it is you need in that report (quarterly figures, regional breakdowns, etc.) and have him redo the report. You may even choose to have a more experienced employee "mentor" Alfred, showing him what needs to be done to improve his work performance. As an employer, it's usually easier to work with someone on improving performance than to start all over again with a new hire.

7. *RELIABILITY* - Just as you value reliability in an employee, it is extremely important to demonstrate and communicate to your employees (with words and actions) that you are a reliable person. Is what you say what you do? If you expect people to accept your vision of the company's future, it is of the utmost importance that you communicate to your employees that you can be relied upon.

When I call the references of people who have expressed a desire to purchase a franchise from

Kitchen Solvers, I always ask, "Is this the kind of person who follows through on what he says he is going to do?" I would much rather be associated with people who show me what they can do rather than with those who tell me what they are going to do...maybe. This is definitely one of those areas where our actions speak louder than words.

Being reliable does not necessarily mean that you will never make any choice or decision that does not turn out well. In fact, for a business owner to become successful, it is almost inevitable that you will make bad decisions along the way. Some people say that as a business owner, if you've never made a bad decision then you haven't made *enough* decisions. How you deal with those bad decisions and what you communicate to your employees about them is what is really important. It is critical to let them know you are taking responsibility for any decisions that have turned out poorly. By not attempting to blame everyone else or deflect responsibility, you are communicating strength of character. You are also communicating to your employees that it is acceptable for them to make decisions that do not always turn out for the best.

A young businessman was going to take over management of a large, successful corporation. On the day before taking over the reins, he thought he would pay a call on the retiring general manager. He knocked on the older gentleman's office door and asked if he had any words of wisdom for him.

The retiring executive, a man of few words, looked at him before he answered.

"Two words—Good decisions."

The young executive thought, "Yes, I can understand that making good decisions would be important for anyone who was to be responsible for managing a large corporation. However, hoping that the man would tell him more, he asked another question. "Sir, how do I learn how to make good decisions?"

"One word—Experience."

Once again, the younger man was somewhat surprised by the brevity of the answer. Yet he knew that he was in the presence of someone who had successfully demonstrated that he could run a large corporation and run it well. So he thought he would ask one more question. "Sir, how do you suggest I acquire the experience needed to make good decisions?"

"Two words. Bad decisions."

---

8. *GOALS* - I would be remiss if I didn't say something about how important it is for a business owner, employer, manager, or supervisor to communicate specific short-term and long-term goals to the staff. To use a football game as an analogy, the short-term goals of the game are to make a series of first downs, to hold the opposition to fewer points, not to make penalties, etc. The long-term goal of the game is to WIN! The short-term goals of your business are to increase sales, to manufacture a quality product, to deliver timely service. The long-term goal of business is to be successful.

In order to make your goals mean something and to encourage the possibility of others accepting those goals, it is also important to provide some incentive for your people when the company's goals are realized. A goal with an incentive provides encouragement for those working for you to work hard and encourage each other.

We recently held our annual convention for Kitchen Solvers' franchises. One of the seminars was conducted by our highest volume franchise, John and Carrie Bordenkircher from Dayton, Ohio. They shared with all of the attendees how they establish goals for their organization, how well their staff and employees participate in and work hard at achieving a common goal, and some of the incentives they use when they establish those goals. After attending the seminar, one of our other franchises, Greg and Darcy Dullum from Gig Harbor, Washington, went home from the convention intent on implementing some goals of their own. They carefully considered what they thought was a goal that would challenge them yet still be achievable, and then tied some staff incentives to that goal. In this case, they told their employees that 1% of the total volume of sales would revert to the employees, a tangible "thank you" for working together to increase business. Greg called me a few days later with the news that he couldn't believe how much his staff had accepted and understood the goals, and how excited they were about putting in the effort necessary to make the vision a reality.

This is a form of communication that can create a win-win situation. Like the old TV commercial once said, "Try it, you'll like it!"

Business Partners

Over the past twenty years I have had almost twenty business partners. (Gee, that sounds like I'm difficult to work with!) Each case was unique, varied in terms of business structure, percentage of ownership, and personal interaction. The majority of those partnering experiences have been very successful. In one case, I have had a 50/50 partner for fifteen years—Mike Tully—and in those fifteen years, we have never shared a cross or negative word with each other. As impossible as that may seem, I believe how we communicated with each other about concerns, responsibilities, finances, etc., and the mutual respect we have had for each other is what made this successful business relationship a reality.

Having business partners lends itself to establishing and maintaining a unique relationship. Growing and developing a successful business partnership has characteristics that are very similar to those necessary to build a good marriage. As with any successful personal relationship, communication is a key ingredient to success.

As we discussed in earlier chapters, before a man and woman exchange marriage vows with each other, it is very important that they have a period of courtship, a time of "getting to know you." If they want to increase the likelihood of enjoying a successful marriage, they must use this courtship time to communicate strengths, weaknesses, likes, and dislikes to each other, as well as the manner in which they will resolve conflicts when they occur.

The same holds true for business relationships. Before anyone enters into a business partner relationship, it is essential that he/she communicates with the other person about the assets and liabilities each one will bring to the table and about each one's expectations for the venture.

Let's say Amy and Sara are opening a web design business. Each one is talented in the field, each one has cash to fund the initial operation, and each one is enthusiastic about the venture. Yet Amy is seeking to augment her husband's income while Sara has quit her previous job and is counting on the business being successful in order for her to make a living. Both women will bring different sets of priorities, strategies and emotions to the venture. They both want it to succeed and they need to discuss common goals and differing opinions well in advance of actually beginning the business.

Also critical to the pre-partnership relationship is determining what responsibilities each party will have and how they will resolve conflicts when they occur. Notice I did not say "if" they occur, but "when." As is true in a marriage relationship, it is virtually impossible never to have issues arise in a business relationship about which you wouldn't have disagreements. In actuality or in principle, choices and decisions will be made that require compromises. Good communication between people in a business venture insures that those compromises will be well thought out and instrumental in making that business relationship successful.

When discussions about starting a business first take place between two or more people, the initial conversation usually centers around a product or service that will generate a profit for all parties involved and how to market that product or service.

Then comes the tough part. Before making any personal or financial commitments to each other, it is essential that all parties involved communicate their expectations for roles and responsibilities with each other. Who will do what, and what time commitments are required? If each party involved has equal ownership, it is crucial that each person has equal responsibilities and time commitments. Most failed business partnerships are the result of one or both parties feeling as if they have more responsibilities or are making more of a time commitment than their counterparts.

Before any two people decide to go into business together, they should first evaluate how compatible their communication skills are. This is not to say they should be identical—simply compatible. In other words, do they understand each other and are they able to communicate clearly to each other about key issues?

In Amy and Sara's case, Amy's strong suit was organization and follow-up, while Sara could "sell ice to Eskimos." They determined that Sara would market the business through sales calls and publicity, while Amy did the "behind-the-scenes" work on accounts. Together, they worked out job responsibility assignments so that there would be a smooth meshing of their talents, with shared time commitments and financial rewards.

Trusting your prospective business partner is another element that is essential to communicate during the "courtship" period. Successful business partnerships are built on mutual trust and respect, and if there is any sense of distrust between you and that person, it is best to walk away from the venture before it gets started. Trust and respect are not the kinds of emotions that grow and evolve as the business partnership grows and matures. They must be there before the venture begins, or you will have trouble sooner or later. Anyone who thinks "well, we can smooth out those wrinkles after we get up and running" will find success hard to achieve and hold onto.

Trust and respect can be communicated to one another both verbally and non-verbally. Personally, I always paid more attention to the non-verbal communication of reliability and dependability of my potential business partners than I did to what they said. For example, prior to becoming a business partner, Mike Tully served as property manager for my income property company. During that period, I was able to observe his performance on a daily basis and it never failed to impress me. Tasks assigned were completed on or ahead of schedule. Sensitive negotiations were handled with discretion and thoughtfulness. Collection of rents and other financial dealings were always done in a professional manner. I knew he would be a good, dependable business partner, one who shared my concerns and philosophies.

Finances

Pay close attention to what your prospective business partner is communicating about his or her attitude about money and finances. What kind of financial expectations does he/she have? Do you have any idea about how personal finances are managed? If married, does he or she communicate to the spouse about money issues, and is he/she living within means?

As in a marriage relationship, financial issues play a prominent role in business partnerships. It is essential that you be up front and open in your communication regarding these matters. Ask questions about the availability of cash input, should it be required.

To communicate about finances after the partnership has been formed may be too late.

How Do They Communicate with Others?

If your prospective business venture requires that your business partner(s) communicates with other people, it would be very important for you to observe *how* he/she does so before "tying the knot."

Before I finalized any of my plans, I observed my potential business partners in numerous social and business settings. I took special notice of how they communicated with other people and how people responded to them. Were they sensitive to the feelings of others? Were they kind or curt in their responses? Did they have a sense of humor? Could they laugh at themselves? Did they interrupt people? Did they cut people off? Were they able to make and maintain eye contact? Positive responses to all these questions were important to me. After all, I was entrusting part of my future to them and to our potential venture.

Conflict Resolution

Prior to beginning any business partnership, I would communicate to my soon-to-be partner that it was important for us to discuss methods for resolving areas of conflict. I recall several occasions when I would raise the issue of conflict resolution and my potential partners were surprised that I wanted to talk about conflicts since we didn't have any at the time. I always explained that it was important to me for this matter to be resolved before any problems occurred. It was necessary to have a clear and mutual understanding of how we would handle decisions when we disagreed, as inevitably we would.

Dissolving a Business Partnership

Sometimes it may be necessary to end a business partnership venture. Perhaps partners discovered they simply couldn't work together any longer. Or maybe the venture is growing unsuccessful and should be closed. Whatever the reasons, if the dissolution is involuntary, it is important that you communicate with caution! Talk about issues rather than personalities because focusing on personalities will only add tension to what is a bad situation. After all, this business partnership may have represented your hopes and dreams for a successful business, and to have it end on an unpleasant note is bound to cause pain to one or both parties.

Selling

There is another entity involved in your business communications, one that is with you whether you are an employee, employer or business partner, and that is *Selling*.

Selling a product, service, concept, or even yourself to an employment office is at the core of every business. What and how we communicate to prospective customers will, indeed, determine how successful we are in sales.

While growing up, going to school, and working as a social worker/marriage and family counselor, I never thought much about the business of selling. I didn't wonder whether or not I could sell anything or if I would enjoy selling as a career. Even when I used to dream about owning a business of my own, I never considered what an important role selling would play.

Then came Kitchen Solvers and it hit me square in the face. Selling and how we communicate with our customers—past, present and future—is critical to the success of a business venture. I also discovered, almost to my surprise, that I enjoyed selling. There was something exhilarating about making a sale, something I experienced with the first three sales calls I made!

As I continued to have success in this new role, I began to ask myself what I liked about selling and what I thought was contributing to my success. After all, I had never taken any sales training classes, nor had anyone instructed me on how to successfully contract with someone to remodel their kitchen! What I discovered was short and simple. I enjoyed meeting new people and I communicated well with those new acquaintances.

After we began franchising, I realized that I would have to focus on my thoughts and techniques about selling so that I could communicate those successful techniques to our new franchise operators. It was important that they attain success in sales. We were investing time, reputation and financial support with these franchises—their success would be our success.

First of all, the person who wants to be successful in sales should enjoy meeting people and making new acquaintances. When I was on sales calls, it was as if I were about to establish a new friendship. People are interesting and there is always something to be learned from a new acquaintance. But what is important to sales success in a business is what those people can learn from you!

Honesty – Whether or not your prospective customers think you are an honest person, someone to be trusted, goes a long way toward making the sale. Naturally, the best way to make other people think that being honest is important to you is to actually BE honest. If a customer asks you a question to which you do not know the answer, say so. Then assure them you will get an answer for them – and do it!

Interest – Do you project a sincere interest in your customer? Think back to our discussion about the "**FORM** method" in Chapter Four. The best way to show interest in others, including prospective customers, is to ask them questions about their **F**amily, **O**ccupation and **R**ecreational interests. How they answer those questions will give you a **M**essage about what they are like. It helps set the tone for the rest of the meeting, establishing common bonds (similar recreational interests, hobbies, friends, etc.) that, in turn, will strengthen the relationship and increase the likelihood of making a sale.

Confidence – How well you communicate a sense of confidence in what you are selling is critical to your success. The best way to communicate this type of confidence is to have a positive opinion about the product or service you are selling and to convey that opinion coherently and concisely.

Rehearse in your mind and aloud what and how you want to get your points across when you are making a sale. Practice with someone else. Ask for constructive criticism from them. After you have gone on a few sales calls, critique yourself. Were you communicating to your customers what you hoped to communicate, or were you getting distracted and off-track? How did they react or respond to points you were trying to make? Did you feel as if you made a positive connection to them? What did you say and could you have said it better?

When I first started selling, I tried to think of every question my prospective customer could ask me. Then I tried to think of good answers to those questions and I rehearsed my delivery until I was comfortable and informed, not merely reciting facts and figures, but understanding what I was selling and to whom I was selling.

Enthusiasm – We've all had experience with salespeople who showed absolutely no interest in their jobs, seemingly annoyed with you when you asked a question, and clueless about the product/service they were selling. At the opposite end of the spectrum, we've seen people who appear eager to help you, informed about their products/services, upbeat and confident about themselves and their jobs. I'm sure that you, like me, much prefer those individuals who carry an aura of enthusiasm for their work. I've even been known to buy something I really didn't need just because the sales presentation was fun and entertaining.

If you are in sales and find it difficult to communicate enthusiasm for your work, maybe you should look for different products/services to represent, or perhaps you should even evaluate whether you should be in sales.

Reliability – Reliability is another important characteristic of a successful sales person, and you communicate reliability by following through on everything you say you are going to do. Not just *some* of the things, but *everything!*

Communicating reliability starts with being on time. Showing up for appointments at the scheduled time, delivering a product or service when you said you would, having answers to customer's questions when promised – all of this says you care about your customer, the sale, and the work you do. There are times, of course, when circumstances make it impossible to be on time, but in this age of cell phones, it is simple and convenient to make a courtesy call informing people of the delay and apologizing.

Listening – An important part of good communication in our personal and social lives is listening, and it is no less true in business and sales. It is crucial that we listen to what our customers are saying. What are they looking for in our products/service? What is important to them? I have observed several of our franchises on sales calls, and in most cases, have been very impressed. However, there have been occasional instances when the salespeople just were not listening. They hear the customer say they want a light cherry stain on the Mission-style cabinetry, but they continue to promote something different.

I've also seen people trying to make the sale long after the customer has already indicated clearly they are sold!

LISTEN, LISTEN, LISTEN! That's the only way you can *hear* what your customer is saying.

As you can see, selling is communication. Whether you are selling new kitchen counters to homeowners, new phone service to a business, or chocolate mint cookies for the Girl Scouts, successful selling comes through successful communication!

Negative Communication

If you own a business and are fortunate enough to have your business succeed, communicating well with customers and employees has most likely been a contributing factor. However, what other people are saying or communicating about you and your success can be very interesting. There certainly will be those who will communicate to you and to others praise for your good fortune. However, as a note of warning or affirmation to existing or aspiring-to-be successful entrepreneurs, you must be wiling to accept the fact that there will be individuals who, behind your back, will communicate to others how they somehow think you cheated or stole your way to your level of success. Some of those people may even be your friends and/or relatives. Regretfully, there are a small percentage of people who have exercised dishonest practices to positively leverage themselves. Nevertheless, I am quite certain that the majority of people who have become financially successful have done so as the result of hard work, determination, commitment, setting goals and exercising good communication.

Someone once told me, when referring to a negative aspect of becoming successful, that the higher up the ladder you are, the more your rear end is exposed. He, of course, was referring to the fact that some people like to take aim, whether justified or not, at the integrity of those who are more successful than they. I believe that negative and false criticism directed toward successful people communicates a number of things about the accuser. First of all, it appears to me that invalid statements that are not based on fact communicate a sense of jealousy and envy. It also communicates, in many cases, a lack of understanding and appreciation for the multiple facets and dynamics that are essential in keeping a business afloat.

Let me share with you a personal example of what I am talking about. While Betty and I were on vacation in Mexico this past year, my name was linked unfavorably in a local newspaper article. A recent fire in a rental unit that I had owned seven years ago prompted the writer to implicate me in her article. She implied that, as a former landlord, I was possibly to blame for code violations and faulty wiring, leading to the fire. She insinuated that I was guilty of putting tenants' lives in danger. She also accused me of failing to respond to her phone call, which was totally untrue. I had e-mailed her, giving her my e-mail address and a phone number in Mexico where she could reach me.

This public accusation bothered me a great deal, which leads me to my main point. Be thoughtful and careful about unleashing negative communication about someone unless you are certain of the facts and that the facts would warrant any harmful or demeaning statements.

CHAPTER EIGHT

IN OTHER WORDS

A Quick Glance at Other Forms of Communication

He could **lead** if he would get the **lead** out.

A farm can **produce** excellent **produce**.

The **present** is a good time to **present** the present.

At the Army base, a **bass** was painted on the head of the **bass** drum.

I did not **object** to the **object**.

The insurance for the **invalid** was **invalid**.

The bandage was **wound** tightly around the **wound**.

They were **too close to** the door of the **clothes** closet **to close** it.

A buck **does** funny things when the **does** are around.

I had to **subject** the **subject** to a series of tests.

I spent last **evening evening** out a pile of dirt.

And people wonder why we often have trouble communicating??

In Other Words

Ever since humans began interacting with each other, communication has existed and allowed us to grow. Whether it was the early cave dwellers who carved pictures on the walls, adventuresome explorers who came upon unknown civilizations, or everyday people who shared a smile and a handshake, communication has existed in many forms.

Written Words as Communication

There are more books than I care to think about that are written about...writing! Business writing, college writing, creative writing. The written word is a powerful tool and one you should always be using, and I urge you to pick up one or two good guides that address the mechanics of writing.

I only want to mention one or two forms of written communication that can impact many of the relationships we have already discussed in prior chapters.

CARDS – Greeting card companies have made life easier for people who have a difficult time expressing themselves in person. There are cards for every conceivable occasion (and many you probably never thought of!). I feel strongly that cards should be chosen with the recipient in mind. If Aunt Thelma is rather reserved and conservative, a birthday card with a suggestive punchline may be funny to you, but she may find it offensive. A sympathy card that is overly emotional may be inappropriate for a business associate or employee. Just as you should think about your words before you open your mouth, you should think about the impact of the card you send before you ever drop it in the mail. Remember, give more attention to how your card will make the recipient feel than how you feel about sending it. To do otherwise would be self-serving.

THANK YOU NOTES - Did your parents make you sit down after you received a birthday or holiday gift and write a thank you note to the sender? It is a habit that many adults seem to grow out of, and they shouldn't. We should still send a thank you note to a distant relative for a pair of socks as well as a thank you card for something special someone did for us. In an earlier chapter we spoke about taking someone you admire to lunch. If that isn't practical, or if it makes you uncomfortable, then why not write a note to that person, thanking him or her for the part he or she has played in your life. A friend of mine, upon hearing of her favorite professor's retirement from college teaching, wrote him a three-page letter recalling the fun she'd had in his class and how his teaching had impacted not only her career choice, but also her way of life. She, in turn, received a heartfelt "thank you" from him! He said retirement had left him feeling a little depressed, but her letter had cheered him up and reminded him why he had gone into teaching to start with.

Thank you notes do not always have to be about big events. They do not even have to be "thank you's"! A note to a neighbor telling her how beautiful her garden looks, a congratulatory note to a business associate upon a promotion, a "well-done" to a child who gets a good grade, even a quick love letter to your spouse—they are all ways of communicating with people and telling them that the relationship is important to you. They will appreciate it, and it will make you feel good too.

RSVP – Call me an etiquette dinosaur, but there are far too many people today who show poor manners and a lack of consideration by their lack of response to an RSVP. RSVP is the abbreviation for the French "Respondez, s'il vous plait," which translates to "Please reply." The idea behind the inclusion of an RSVP card, phone number or even e-mail address, is to advise the host/hostess of your attendance at an event, a dinner, a party, etc. Usually, a great deal of time, effort, expense and planning goes into an event, whether it is a small social gathering or a large business event, and the people behind that planning appreciate knowing how many guests will be there.

Please, next time you receive anything containing an RSVP, check your calendar and respond within a day or two. Your hosts will appreciate it! (And if you find it necessary to cancel, make sure you call—not write—and deliver your regrets!) Emily Post and I will rest easier.

The Sense of Touch as Communication

The use of touch is a wonderful communication enhancer. When you are trying to communicate feelings of warmth and friendship with words and you add the sense of touch, you multiply the effect. Appropriately touching someone on the arm, shoulder, hand or back conveys a feeling of sincerity, strengthening the connection between you and the other person. Obviously, it is important to use good judgment in how often you use this communication technique, and you should be particularly sensitive to any signs of discomfort from the other person. There are some people who feel uncomfortable when you touch them, so you should proceed cautiously.

One indication of the effectiveness of touch in establishing positive relationships comes from a study that was recently completed at the University of Miami School of Medicine. It showed that fathers who made a habit of touching their infant children were able to establish warm and positive relationships that deepened as the children grew. We are all very much like those infants—an appropriate touch from people we trust is reassuring for us and leads to better relationships.

When dealing with adults, it may be helpful to observe people around you. Watch those whom you admire in various settings. Do they use the art of touching in social conversations, business meetings, family gatherings? It always interests me to watch different people in the same setting. One man may lay his hand on my forearm when he wants to emphasize a point, while another may tap his finger on my chest to make the same point. You can experiment with this form of communication to see if you will be comfortable with it.

The same applies to hugging. Our family is a family of huggers and it spills over into social situations for me. There are some friends who feel comfortable hugging, while others I know feel slightly hesitant about it. To me, it is simply an indication of the warmth and affection I have for those friends, something I can never communicate to them too much.

CHAPTER NINE

ALI MACGRAW WAS WRONG!

The Importance of Learning to Say "I'm Sorry."

I'm Sorry

In the 1970 hit movie *Love Story*, the main character, played by Ali MacGraw, assured her husband that "Love means never having to say you're sorry." Maybe so, but being *able* to say "I am sorry" plays a very important role in the relationship between husband and wife. It is also a critical component in the success of relationships between parent and child, employer and employee, friends and friends.

Due to the simple dynamic of any relationship—two people communicating and exchanging thoughts, feelings, emotions—it is almost impossible not to experience some conflicts. More than likely something will occur, either significant or not, that will hurt or offend your spouse, child, parent, relative, co-worker, or friend. When that happens, are you able to say "I am sorry"? If and when you do say those very important words, do you mean them? It can honestly be said that "I am sorry" is among the most important and powerful phrases that anyone can communicate.

Every meaningful relationship has its peaks and valleys. Saying "I am sorry" can be the bridge for successfully getting you through the valleys that will inevitably occur. I have heard some people say that it is very hard for them to say "I am sorry." If you are one of those people, have you ever asked yourself why? If you struggle with those three words, you probably have already experienced the negative consequences from not being able to apologize.

Apologizing is not a sign of weakness. Quite the contrary. Making that apologetic gesture and delivering a sincere "I am sorry" is a real sign of strength. There is a distinct correlation between people who have low self-esteem and those who cannot admit their mistakes and take responsibility for them. If it is difficult for you to communicate those three words in person to someone, write a letter or make a phone call. Just do it!

In most relationships, it is usually more difficult for one person to say "I am sorry" than for the other. That's okay. But it is not okay to leave a blank in this very important part of your relationship.

In our marriage, Betty is better and faster at saying "I'm sorry" than I am. She is very quick to recognize when her words or behavior have had a negative impact and attempt to make amends. It takes me a little longer, but I usually come through.

And we always seal the settlement with a hug and a kiss.

If you're convinced you're right and simply will not or cannot apologize to your spouse, try apologizing for the bad feeling. There's a big difference between "I'm sorry I can't stand your sister" and "I'm sorry that my not being able to stand your sister has made you feel bad."

Something my parents instilled in their kids was that you should never say goodbye or goodnight without resolving disagreements or "clearing the air." I recall my mother asking us many times, "How would you feel if you died in your sleep or a car accident and the last time you spoke it was in anger?"

It is also important, when looking at the value and meaning of saying "I am sorry," that you never keep track of how many times you say the words. Repeat those words until you know that the other person believes you mean it. This is not an athletic event and you cannot keep score. If you do, both parties lose. And once that apology is made and accepted, move on. Don't dwell on it, either as apologizer or apologizee—life is too short!

One of the more difficult things for a parent to do is to apologize to a young child or teen-ager. Perhaps it is the basic parent-as-teacher structure of our relationships to our children that makes it awkward. After all, aren't we supposed to have all the answers and know exactly what is right and wrong? Why would we need to tell a child "I'm sorry"? And yet saying those words to a child is teaching a valuable lesson, one that a child will profit from all of his or her life.

Saying "I'm sorry" to a child not only demonstrates that we are all fallible, all capable of being wrong, but it shows a child that apologizing does not diminish the person making the apology. It may even allow for further dialogue with the child. "I'm sorry I yelled at you earlier, Tommy. I should have found a better way to express my anger. Do you ever get that mad at someone?"

As long as we're discussing being able to say "I'm sorry" to a child, this might be the appropriate place to say something about being able to apologize to *adult* children. As you examine your parenting history, if you discover and accept the fact that you may have made some major blunders in what you said or did to your children in the past, try to make amends. It is never too late to present your adult children with an apology.

Please don't misunderstand. I don't want you filled with guilt and recriminations, because we have all made mistakes as parents. But if there is something that still haunts you— something that may be standing in the way of you having a strong and loving relationship with your children—then go and apologize. I can assure you, if it still haunts you, your children have not erased it from their memories either, and your relationship will be all the stronger for having said "I'm sorry."

Saying "I'm sorry" can play a significant role in the workplace also. Imagine that you are responsible for compiling a monthly sales report, something that requires reports from four other people in your department. One person doesn't have her report in on time, forcing you to be late with your report. Which of the following would you prefer to hear from that co-worker? *"Ed, here are those numbers you needed. Give me a call if you have any questions.*" Or… "*Ed, here are those numbers you needed. I apologize for the delay because I know that held you up in getting your report done. I've already let Mr. Hampton know it was my fault.*" The employee who takes responsibility for his or her actions on the job indicates two things to co-workers: first, that he or she realizes the problem that resulted from an incident, and, secondly, that such an awareness of the problem may prevent it from happening again.

Similarly, an employer who has made a mistake reflects a sincere consideration for his or her employees when an apology is forthcoming. "*Jerry, I know I should have given you more warning about that plant inspection. I apologize for ruining your weekend and I appreciate the extra hours you put in for us.*" As I've said earlier, being able to apologize is a sure sign of strength and concern.

Right now—at this moment—can you think of something for which you need to say "I am sorry" to someone? Please do it. You'll be amazed at how good it makes that person feel. And you'll be even more amazed at how good it makes you feel!

Bridge That Gap!

Something that is closely associated with the idea of being able to say "I'm sorry" is the concept of burning bridges. Burning bridges is when one person says or does something that discourages another person from ever wanting to have or continue a relationship with that person. It can take place in social, family or business relationships with equally destructive results. It might occur when two people are communicating with each other and perhaps harsh words are exchanged.

Misunderstandings can lead to hurt feelings that snowball into angry conversations and next thing you know, a relationship is cooled or even ended. Voila! A burned bridge.

I'm not sure if my parents intentionally taught me the value of not burning bridges or if I learned simply from observation. All I know is that it was something I always sought to avoid and still do to this day. There are few cases where burning a bridge ever brought about positive results. And yet some people see it as the only action they can take. They tend to stockpile what I call BB's, or "burning bridge" ammunition, recalling the exact words or gestures that fostered bad feelings, intentionally throwing their own BB's into the fire to create an uncomfortable or hostile environment. There may be no way to avoid having these feelings, but self-restraint is the best bet. Harbor the thoughts, if you must, but sit on the words and actions. The minimal satisfaction you may receive from communicating exactly how you feel is just not worth the potential damage that it can cause later in your life.

To tie back into the "I'm sorry" aspect of this chapter, keep in mind that it is almost always possible to repair a damaged relationship, to keep that bridge intact. It requires strong character and a positive determination to do it, but it is possible.

Have you got a burned bridge relationship in your life? Is it one that still causes you regret and pain? Go to that person and say you are sorry. Again, you do not need to say you are sorry for the words that were exchanged, but for the *result* of those words. *"I'm sorry that what I said made you feel we could no longer be friends. I never meant for that to happen, and I wish there was*

a way we could repair our friendship—it means a lot to me."
The problem may not be cured overnight, but the boards have
been put in place to try to build a new relationship bridge.

For me, the meaning and significance of being able to say, "I am
sorry" is so high that I would like to put together a book on that
topic alone. You can help.

Please send me a letter describing your personal experience,
either in marriage, family, social, or business, where saying or
not saying "I am sorry" has had a positive or negative impact on
your life. Perhaps your story could help someone else.
Information for submitting letters can be found at the back of the
book. Thanks!

CHAPTER TEN

HEY, I KNOW YOU!!

Celebrity Communicators

The President of the United States, A Nobel Prize winner, the Pope, and a Boy Scout happened to be on a small plane that was going down, and alas, as jokes will have it, there were only three parachutes available.

The President of the United States announced, "I am President of the United States, leader of the free world, and I must survive for world peace." He then grabbed a parachute and jumped from the plane.

The Nobel Prize winner announced that "I was just awarded a Nobel Prize for being the smartest man in the world and I must survive so that people may benefit from my great intelligence." He then grabbed a parachute and jumped from the plane.

The Pope turned to the Boy Scout and said, "My son, I am old and nearing death anyway. You take the last parachute and save yourself."

The Boy Scout smiled and said, "That's okay, Your Eminence, the smartest man in the world just jumped out with my knapsack."

Fame does not guarantee success!!

Good Communication Brings Celebrity Status

John D. Rockefeller once said, *"People skills are a learned skill, and I will pay more for that skill than any other."*

In an attempt to gain a clearer picture of how good communication contributes to successful living, I thought it would be interesting to evaluate the communication skills of some very successful people. People skills and one's ability to communicate play a very important role in elevating someone to celebrity status. I have selected four very well-known people and have tried to examine the communication skills these individuals possess. Also, when conducting the surveys referenced in the Introduction, all interviewees were asked what communication skills they thought these celebrities had that contributed to their success. See if you agree or disagree with the characteristics we have assigned.

David Letterman – Mr. Letterman is the host of *Late Night With David Letterman* on CBS, watched every evening by millions of people. Everyone I interviewed felt that his ability to see humor in insignificant events and his ability to laugh at himself were his special trademarks. Most felt that he was a good listener, asking good questions to draw out his guests. His ability to think and react quickly is an innate communication skill that he was blessed with. While some people thought he could be abrasive at times, they also felt that he was able to get away with it because of the whimsical method in which it was expressed. He appears to have a sincere interest in other people and is quick to determine what people like to talk about. His relaxed style contributes to the general impression that he is who he is. In other words, what you see is what you get with David Letterman.

Words are certainly not the only method of communication he uses. Facial expressions and body language are great communication enhancers, and his ability to utilize both solicits a lot of laughter from his audience.

Timing was another characteristic that several people assigned to Letterman. Timing is a difficult skill to describe or imitate, but, in general, it is one's ability to know when to say something (or when not to), when to tease someone or to make fun of oneself.

I suspect that Letterman has critiqued his style most of his life. As a former writer, he learned to use words and communication, and it has helped him become a household name. With only one exception, everyone I interviewed liked to watch David Letterman and would place him at the top of the list of successful comedians.

Bill Clinton – While it was difficult for those I interviewed not to express their political viewpoints of Mr. Clinton, most agreed that his communication skills were ranked highly. Charisma certainly plays a significant role in his style of communication and, in spite of his moral missteps, I think history will remember him as the President with the most charisma.

Clinton's command of the English language gives him the ability to communicate with everyone at their level. Most felt that his ability to sustain eye contact and his ability to focus on what was being discussed were very successful communication skills for him. Maintaining good eye contact makes a person feel special, as if for those few moments he or she is the only one who matters.

President Clinton was also described as appearing to be a good listener, one who communicates very well his concern for other people. The quality of his voice communicates compassion for others, and his ability to think and communicate logically helped maintain his popularity.

I was reminded of Mr. Clinton's positive communication skills as I observed my parents' shift in political party alliance. For as long as I can remember, both of them were Republicans, so to one day hear them endorsing Bill Clinton was quite a surprise. When I asked which political decision or policy of Clinton's made them switch, they were unable to be specific, but finally admitted it was because they liked to watch him on TV. He was certainly a politician who recognized the power of television and directed his communication skills towards the camera when needed.

Bill Clinton has an incredible talent of communicating emotions and, consequently, makes himself appear very sincere.

The overall attitude of those who participated in my interview was that President Clinton's communication skills enhanced his ability to get his message across to other people and have, without a doubt, assured him a spot in history as a strong communicator.

Oprah Winfrey - Oprah Winfrey has carved out for herself a special place in the television and movie industry. When I asked people to tell me what they considered her most important communication skills, almost everyone pointed to her non-threatening, non-judgmental personality and her easy-going style.

In spite of her celebrity status, she has maintained her ability to "be herself," overcoming numerous personal obstacles in her life. That sense of her "weathering the storm" and being able to share those experiences with her audience has raised her credibility with many people.

She communicates a sincere concern for others, being described as a very good listener with an ability to ask solid, thought-provoking questions that many viewers would ask in her place. Many people commented on her lack of pretensions and her overall impression of honesty.

Personality characteristics of being reliable and trustworthy make it easy for her guests and audience members to be open with her. She communicates a positive mental attitude and, therefore, is a source of motivation and inspiration to others.

Oprah Winfrey's ability to communicate with others and the desire of others to communicate with her have had immeasurable influence on her becoming a media celebrity.

Dr. Robert Schuller – Dr. Robert Schuller has been a staple of Sunday morning television for over 25 years, delivering his messages of faith and hope from California's "Crystal Cathedral." I have watched and listened to him for most of that time. In direct contrast to the "fire-and-brimstone" preachers on many television shows, Dr. Schuller's love and compassion for his God and Jesus Christ are apparent as he puts emphasis on communicating hope and optimism for one's life.

Dr. Schuller's method of communication is definitely upbeat, enthusiastic, positive and optimistic. The consensus was that he communicates honesty and compassion, and that he is genuine in his faith. He has the ability to make you feel as though he is speaking directly to you, and often he gets his points across by sharing true stories and using real-life examples to illustrate his messages.

Other words used to describe Dr. Schuller were warm, understanding, intelligent, comforting, wise, and having good voice fluctuation.

One of the highlights of his Sunday morning worship services is the interview wherein he asks thoughtful questions, listening to the answers very closely, as indicated by his follow-up questions. He shows a sincere interest in the lives of other people, something he may have been born with or learned over time. It is obvious during these interviews that he also uses the sense of touch very effectively to communicate.

Dr. Schuller's communication skills have played a significant role in attracting millions of people around the world to his Christian ministry. It is not so much what he believes in, but how he communicates his message to people that has led to his popularity and to his success.

So what do these four very different individuals have in common that makes them so well-liked and respected by people? After listening to the people I interviewed, I was able to draw several conclusions.

In each case their ability to listen carefully was described as a positive characteristic. They listened to their guests and were able to ask thoughtful questions that not only drew out their guests, but made them feel relaxed and accepted.

All four exuded a comfortable warmth which seemed to make others feel good to be in their presence. They were overwhelmingly positive in their general attitudes and outlooks about life. Pessimism and negativity are not part of their personalities.

The key idea to remember is that you do not have to be a celebrity to make people feel good. Enhancing your communication skills can make you a celebrity in your own relationships, an individual people will respect and whose company they will enjoy.

CHAPTER ELEVEN

THE ULTIMATE RELATIONSHIP

Communicating with God

If Madison Avenue had its way..........

God is a little like General Electric—He lights your way.

God is a little like Bayer aspirin—He works wonders.

God is a little like Hallmark Cards—He cared enough to send the very best.

God is a little like Tide—He gets out the stains that others leave behind.

God is a little like Alberto VO-5 Hair Spray—He holds through all kinds of weather.

God is a little like Dial Soap—Aren't you glad you know Him? Don't you wish everybody did?

God is a little like Sears—He has everything.

God is a little like Alka-Seltzer—Oh, what a relief He is!

God is a little like Scotch tape—You can't see Him, but you know He's there.

God is a little like American Express—Don't leave home without Him!

Amen to it all!!

The Ultimate Relationship

I saved this chapter for the end of the book for several reasons. First of all, I am very conscious about not wanting to force my religious views or opinions on anyone else. I do not think it is wrong for people to share what their relationship to God means to them, but I do feel that it is wrong to judge someone else negatively if his or her opinions do not agree with yours.

It is also a difficult chapter for me to write because I am still trying to define and clarify for myself the depth and understanding of what and how I communicate with God.

When I decided to write a book on communication and thought about how important communication is in our lives, one of the first thoughts I had was "How do we communicate with God?" Those who do not believe in God would question how you *can* communicate with someone you cannot see, hear or touch. You could say that you cannot see the wind either, but you can feel it. You cannot hear, see or touch carbon monoxide, but it can have a deadly effect on you. But no one talks about communicating with the wind or carbon monoxide. So to describe how you communicate with God is a challenging task.

However, I feel that God plays such a very important role in my life that not devoting a chapter to communicating with God would be doing a disservice to a relationship that is the essence of my life.

As I began to write this chapter, I found myself communicating to God by praying, *"Dear God, I ask that You would be with me as I write the words for this chapter. Inspire me to use the right words and thoughts to best describe my relationship with You, how it is that I communicate with You, and how You communicate with me. Grant me the wisdom to adequately communicate my personal relationship to You while remaining sensitive to the opinions and feelings of others."*

Those words do not represent all of my prayer, but they represent the thoughts I was trying to communicate.

Since I am a Christian, I feel like I am speaking to Jesus Christ and God at the same time. For me, Jesus represents the "human" embodiment of God, and I find it easier to communicate *to* God *through* Jesus, as though he is "translating" my thoughts and feelings.

To help explain what this means to me, I would like to share a story with you that former pastor and good friend Vern Rice shared with our congregation one Christmas Eve:

"It was Christmas Eve in a rural community in a part of the country where they experience severe cold weather and heavy snowfalls. Following their Christmas Eve meal, a mother and her three children were readying themselves to drive to their community church to attend the Christmas Eve service. The father chose not to go. While he acknowledged that he believed in the existence of some omniscient power, he did not believe nor accept that God would send someone to earth as a human being to relate to the people of this world.

Shortly after the rest of the family left to attend the service, a violent winter storm erupted without warning. He went to the farmyard to gather all the animals into the shelter of the barn where they would be safe from the freezing snow and driving wind. He got all the animals secured except for the flock of sheep. As hard as he tried, he could not get them to go through the open barn door. He knew that if he did not protect them, they

> would surely freeze to death. He thought to himself, 'If there was just some way for me to communicate to them that their lives are in danger and that I'm trying to help them.' Then he fell to his knees thinking, 'If only I could become one of them, then I would be able to communicate with them and I would be able to save their lives.'"

Jesus became one of us humans in order to be able to share God's message with us. When I am communicating with God, I feel that I am communicating to Him through Jesus Christ. It helps me make that important connection. If you are not a Christian and you want to communicate with God, it is important that you somehow develop for yourself an effective way of having a dialogue.

In all of our relationships, we try to strengthen and maintain them through meaningful and frequent communication. The better communication we have, the better we feel about that person. So it is with God. The better communication we have with Him and the frequency with which we communicate will most likely determine the strength of our relationship to God.

Since communicating with God is unlike most two-way conversations we have in our earthly relationships, we have to be creative in how we make it happen.

As part of a Bible study group in which Betty and I participate, we followed a study guide for several weeks on the Meaning of Prayer. As a part of those discussions, I discovered that it was just as difficult for the other members of the group to define what communicating with God meant for them as it was for me.

Naturally, when most people think or talk about communicating with God, they think about prayer. The concept of prayer implies that you share thoughts, words, requests, thanks, etc. either verbally or non-verbally to the omniscient power in which you believe.

The study guide we all used in our group describes prayer this way: *"Prayer can be private or public, ritualized or conversational, silent or out loud, spoken or sung, words or action, simple or profound. Through prayer, God's will is discerned and greater clarity is gained for our journey. [Prayer] is Adoration (praise, honoring God), Confession (saying, 'I'm sorry,' acknowledging sin and that 'I can't do it on my own'), Thanksgiving (saying thanks, counting blessings, allowing God's perspective to shape life), and Supplication (asking for, praying for others, petitionary in character)."*

from the "Call to Discipleship", a publication of the Evangelical Lutheran Church in America
8765 W. Higgins Rd.
Chicago, IL 60631

If you reflect on some of the most meaningful conversations you have had with the important people in your life, I suspect the setting or atmosphere where those discussions took place played an important role. It might have been some place where it was quiet and you were not interrupted and distracted. So it is in trying to have the most meaningful communication with God. It is important to choose a time and place to help enhance the exchange between you and God.

For me, sitting under the stars and moon at night or atop a towering mountain can make me feel as if I'm on the same frequency as my God. I feel that presence when watching the constant motion of a river, lake or ocean, or looking at breath-taking landscapes of flowers and trees. I suspect the clarity of my dialogue in these settings is best because I have a strong sense that He is there. I feel His presence and, therefore, my communication is more meaningful.

When I communicate with God, I know what I have said to Him, but I am not always sure of what He is trying to say to me. Unlike a few people who have described in believable words how God has spoken directly to them, I wait for His response to me in the form of events or experiences that take place in my life. I don't believe things just happen; instead, there is a reason for many of the events in our lives. I believe that much of what occurs is the answer to prayers previously made. Sometimes what God communicates back to me is not what I asked for or expected. However, because of the omniscience that I have assigned to Him, I accept the unknown fact that He knows what is better for me than I do. And then, of course, there are those numerous occasions when I feel as if He does not respond to my requests, or that I am still waiting for Him to answer.

The Bible is the most widely read book in the world. There has never been another book that comes anywhere close to being read as much or as often as the Bible. If we are to believe that the Bible is the inspired word of God (and I do), then certainly reading the Bible and participating in Bible studies are wonderful ways of trying to understand what God is communicating to us.

In most relationships, we have a reasonably good grasp for whether or not our feelings toward one another are mutual. We gain insight into these emotions by communicating with each other. Even though the method by which we communicate with God is different than with humans, it is still possible to evaluate the depth and meaning of one's relationship to God by the reciprocity of our communication.

Betty and I recently attended a Green Bay Packer (three time winner of the Super Bowl!) football game. As a way of revving up the crowd and getting them excited about the game, the announcer said, "This is our house." Those people in attendance who supported the Packers held a distinct advantage over their opponents because the game was being played within the confines of a facility built for fans to come and cheer their favorite team. (Did I mention that the Packers won the Super Bowl three times?) A church, a mosque, a synagogue or other place of worship is often referred to as "the House of God." Mentally, emotionally, and spiritually, it makes us feel like we are in closer proximity to God and gives more meaning to the words we say when we are guests in God's house. In this "House of God," I feel that the words I share with Him are better understood and I have a stronger sense of what He is trying to communicate to me.

Consider this analogy: If you wanted to develop a meaningful relationship with someone, would you do so only by talking on the telephone, letters or e-mails? Wouldn't you prefer to visit them in their home or invite them to your home and get to know them better? I think the meaning and depth of our communication is heightened by going to the place where our loved ones live.

Attending worship services is very important for me in maintaining and improving my communication with God. I am not implying that it is impossible to communicate with God if you do not go to church; however, going to the House of God and participating with others in prayer, communion, singing and listening to a homily all contribute to the way I can strengthen my relationship with God.

I believe there is another important way we can communicate with God, and that is through the act of giving. Giving of our time, talents and treasure is a meaningful way of communicating our love for Him. I also believe there is a direct correlation between what we give and what we receive. For me, it is impossible to outgive the Giver. As we give, so shall we receive, says the Bible. There is a wonderful quote from Winston Churchill that says "We make a living by what we get, but we make a life by what we give."

Some of you may think that giving to God and communicating with God are far removed from each other, but consider this analogy. If I were to choose a gift for the friend of a friend, I would probably ask someone to help me make a selection, and I would probably limit my spending. On the other hand, if I am buying Betty a birthday, Christmas or anniversary gift, I would take time to find something special myself, and I would spend more because I would be trying to convey or communicate my love for her. Therefore, giving and giving freely is a special form of communication for me to express my love and respect for the God in which I believe.

When I evaluate my own relationship to God, I often think about what I should or should not communicate to others about my beliefs. As best I can, I try to respect the private opinion of others regarding this important and highly personal matter. On the other hand, God has communicated to me through Jesus Christ that He wants us to be fishers of men, which to me means sharing (communicating) with others what I believe. If I have carefully evaluated the situation, on occasion I will tell others what I believe, but the best way I can communicate to others about what I believe is by the way I live my life. On several occasions, people have said to me, "I'll bet you're a Christian." When I respond affirmatively, I always ask them what made them think so, and they usually say words to the effect that it is "because of the way you speak and the way you act." For me, that is the highest compliment anyone could ever give me. I think that it is very important to have a close correlation between the way we conduct our lives and what we believe in. This concept is not only important as it relates to our belief in God, but it is important in all areas of our life.

One last analogy for you. If I held certain political opinions and felt strongly about an issue, yet I supported and voted for a candidate that held an opposing view, what would that tell you? I imagine you would have a difficult time believing other things I told you as well. This is just one more example of our actions speaking louder than our words.

Having written this chapter has helped clarify several things for me:

- I better understand the meaning of my relationship to God;
- It is clearer to me how I communicate with God;
- I have given more consideration about how I communicate my belief in God to others;
- Like other important relationships in my life, I understand more clearly that trying to improve my relationship to God and the way I communicate with Him is an ongoing venture. Meaningful relationships don't die or fade away when we are willing to give to that relationship and if what we expect to get back is realistic.

CHAPTER TWELVE

SUMMARY

So here we are, the last pages. It feels good to be writing the words to the final chapter of my first book. When I first contemplated the idea of writing a book, I was completely unaware of the amount of time and effort required to pull it all together, to go from thoughts and ideas to written words on a page. There were times when I found it difficult to write anything, and there were times when I couldn't write quickly enough to capture everything I wanted to say.

This book represents the completion of a unique task, something I have never done before and, quite frankly, something I was unsure that I would be able to accomplish. However, communication has so much meaning and profound implications on our lives that, once started, I had to keep going.

As I indicated in the Prologue, I understood that you might not agree with everything I said, but I do hope that as you read, you held up that "mental mirror" to your own communication style and thought about it carefully. Good communication has so much value and meaning to those important relationships you have in life that it is really worth the study.

While working on this book, I would often speak with friends and acquaintances about the project and they were always interested in the topic. There are thousands of books aimed at specific interests or hobbies—fishing, computers, bee-keeping, eating habits of the brontosaurus, etc. The people buying those books are as varied as the titles themselves. But communication involves us all. Everyone on earth communicates in some way or another with others on the planet each and every day. How we communicate has a significant impact on the amount of joy and happiness we experience in our lives. I hope I have been able to convey my unwavering philosophy that everyone is capable of improving relationships to others by improving communication with others... IF THEY WANT TO. I work on it every day and will continue to do so. Improving our communication skills should be an unending process.

The exchange of words, thoughts and feelings is key to new and long-term meaningful relationships and the positive result of good communication. Similarly, poor communication has led to many broken relationships. Anyone who dismisses the harmful effects of poor communication need look no further than the daily news to find stories of anger, violence and hostility that resulted from misunderstandings. We do have the ability to control how and what we communicate to others.

Look closely at your own communication skills. Understand that how you communicate can impact not only your own life, but those around you. You may not be able to change how someone else communicates, but you can change your methods and habits. Just imagine what it would be like if all of us were more aware of the impact our words have on people, and took positive steps to be more sensitive and open in our relationships!

I have used "communication" and "communicate" hundreds of times in this book. That is what this book has been all about. So in closing, let me communicate clearly—and from my heart—to you.

- I hope and pray that you are blessed with many meaningful relationships in your life.
- I hope you have enjoyed taking a closer look at the role communication plays in your life.
- And I hope that you agree—good communication skills unlock the doors for successful living.

APPENDIX I

SAMPLE SURVEYS

Communication Survey

Please answer all questions by **circling the one** best answer:

1. Age:

    0-17   18-24   25-35   36-49   50-64   65+

2. Education:

    High School   Some College

    College Graduate   Post Graduate

3. Income Level (if married, joint income):

    0 – $29,000 $30 – 49,000 $50 – 74,000

    $75 – 100,000 $100,000 +

4. Sex: Male   Female

5. Marital Status:

    Single   Married   Divorced   Widowed

6. Number of siblings:

    0   1   2   3   4   5 or more

7. Where do you fit in the family order:

    1st born   middle born   last born

8. Occupation of parents while you were growing up:

Manual Laborer	Professional	Clerical
Management	Business Owner	

---

9. Population of location where you spent the majority of the first 18 years of your life:

0-999	1,000 – 4,000	5,000 – 24,000
25,000 – 99,999	100,000 – 499,999	500,000 +

On a scale of 1 to 10 (with 10 being **very good** and 1 being **very poor**), please rate yourself for the following categories:

Communicating to other people in general

1	2	3	4	5	6	7	8	9	10

Communicating to members of your family

1	2	3	4	5	6	7	8	9	10

Communicating to your employer (if you are currently unemployed, indicate how you felt about relating to any past employer)

1	2	3	4	5	6	7	8	9	10

Communicating to employees (if you have never had employees, there is no need to answer)

1	2	3	4	5	6	7	8	9	10

Communicating to new acquaintances

1   2   3   4   5   6   7   8   9   10

Communicating in small groups

1   2   3   4   5   6   7   8   9   10

Communicating to someone else on a one-to-one basis

1   2   3   4   5   6   7   8   9   10

How good are you at initiating communications to a new acquaintance?

1   2   3   4   5   6   7   8   9   10

If you thought it was possible to improve your communication skills, what would be your level of interest in doing so?

1   2   3   4   5   6   7   8   9   10

How do you feel about people who do not reciprocate in your communication to them? (1 – "it upsets you very much 10 – "it does not bother you at all")

1   2   3   4   5   6   7   8   9   10

How receptive would you be to having someone make suggestions to you about how you could improve your communication skills? (1 – being very unreceptive 10 – being very receptive)

1   2   3   4   5   6   7   8   9   10

Personal Interview Questions

1. Do you think very often about how you communicate with other people and how others communicate with you?

2. Are there certain situations when you find it difficult to communicate? Why?

3. Do you have any jokes about communication?

4. Who is someone that you think is a good communicator and why?

5. What communication skills do the following people possess that you admire?
   a. David Letterman
   b. Bill Clinton
   c. Oprah Winfrey
   d. Rev. Robert Schuller

6. Do you communicate with other people differently than you do with members of your family? If so, why?

7. Who are the most difficult people for you to communicate with? Why?

8. How important is it to you how other people communicate with you?

9. Have you ever made a conscious effort to improve your communication skills?

10. Do you believe it is possible for people to improve upon how they communicate?

11. If you could improve one thing about the way you communicate, what would it be?

APPENDIX II

SURVEY RESULTS

I mentioned in the beginning that in an effort to better understand the meaning and significance of communication in the lives of individuals, I had 187 people complete a general survey. I did not indicate the topic of my book on the survey itself, so interviewees were unaware of the reasons behind the questions. Dr. Robert Morehouse, Professor of Psychology at Viterbo University, administered approximately 90 surveys himself as well as compiling all the results. While this certainly was not a scientific research study, there were some interesting results and I do feel that some of those results are worth noting, along with my personal interpretation of those results.

I chose not to include the statistical results themselves in this book, if for no other reason that it makes for rather dry reading. If you would like to see the statistical report, please make your request to *gerald@kitchensolvers.com* and I will be happy to send you a copy.

The statistical results of the survey seemed to indicate that those individuals with the lowest income (under $30,000/year) and those with the highest income (over $100,000/year) felt the most confident about their overall communication skills. It should be pointed out that the majority of the individuals with a lower than $30,000 income were college students. Generally speaking, they are young people who have just recently left their families and the experience of living at home, and who have had limited experience in the "adult world." My supposition is that they would feel quite strongly about their communication skills because their ability to communicate has not been challenged to the same degree as those individuals who completed the survey who were significantly older.

Further, I would think it logical that those individuals who completed the survey who had the highest income have a great deal of confidence in their communication skills because those skills have contributed to professional success. In other words, "I'm making more money because I'm successful and I'm successful because I have been able to communicate effectively."

The survey results indicated that those individuals born into families where one or both parents were in management or business owners also felt the most confident about their ability to communicate. This might suggest that people coming from these families saw the need for and the benefits of good communication skills in their parents' lives.

Another interesting result that stood out was that individuals who were born into families with parents who held clerical or manual laborer positions rated themselves the highest in terms of their ability to communicate with members of his or her family. Why do you think that might be? Is it possible to make a generalization that families with lower incomes spend more time together as a family than members of higher income families? Research (by others, not me) indicates that lower income families tend to continue living in close proximity to their extended families than do professional people who often move to different locations as they seek job advancement. Maybe they feel they communicate better because they simply communicate more often with family members. Practice makes perfect???

Those individuals with the highest income indicated the most willingness to improve their communication skills, and were open to someone making suggestions about how they could improve those skills. It would suggest that those people who have attained a degree of success in their careers recognize the value of good communication skills and are always seeking to improve those skills.

As indicated before, this was not a scientific study. Nevertheless, I did find it interesting to contemplate and reflect on some of the results.

As I mentioned in Chapter Nine, I would like to gather examples of personal experiences when saying "I'm sorry" made an impact—negative or positive—on my readers' lives.

If you have an example you would like to share (hopefully to help someone else), please send it to me at:

Gerald Baldner
Kitchen Solvers
401 Jay St.
La Crosse, WI 54601

Or e-mail your story to me at:
gerald@kitchensolvers.com

If you would like to have Mr. Baldner speak at your convention, deliver a keynote address at a banquet, or provide consultation services for your company, please contact him at 608-791-5519 or e-mail him at gerald@kitchensolvers.com

Notes

Notes

Notes